LESSONS
from the
BATTLEFIELD

LESSONS
from the
BATTLEFIELD

John Henson

Commendations

Lessons from the Battlefield is one of the most honest and frank accounts of the life of a pastor I have been privileged to read. In days when many work hard to maintain a facade about public ministry, but struggle in private, John has articulated something of the journey he and Clare have travelled with an honesty that is refreshing. The lessons that John expounds travel well from the context of his ministry in southern Africa too, reminding us that people and circumstances vary very little across the body of Christ in the world today. I recommend this work to you, especially if you are, like John and I, Pastors at heart. Within it you will find encouragement to see God at work in the ordinary moments and everyday circumstances that are the very field in which we shepherd God's people.

Rev Stuart Blount
Director of Ministry, Elim Churches UK

There are those who are of the opinion that spiritual leaders should not share their challenges and struggles publicly. That view is not however supported by Scripture. The only way that we can be made aware of the debilitating effects of Jesus being tempted in the wilderness, at the commencement of His earthly ministry, and the anguish of Gethsemane at the end, is because the Son of God was willing to share what had happened with His disciples – given that in both cases He was alone at the time. Taking that as a template the writer of this book with transparency, honesty and vulnerability shares his story for the same reason that Jesus shared His, according to Hebrews 2:18, so that others can profit from it.

Rev John Glass
Former General Superintendent, Elim Churches UK
Author of 'Building Bigger People'

This book offers honest insights into real life situations that many people will face in ministry. It will allow you to reflect on an others experience, inspiring you to seek God for wisdom to navigate the battles and blessings that life brings...

Rev David Newton
Director of Training and Principal Regents Theological College

Dedication

Dedicated to my dear wife Clare, and my sons Michael, Timothy and David who have shared this adventure with me. Also to all who have heeded the Master's call and have denied themselves, taken up their crosses, and followed our Good, Great and Chief Shepherd in His ministry.

Copyright © John Henson July 2016
ISBN 978-1-907929-75-5

Contact: johnhenson14@aol.co.uk

Life Publications
www.lifepublications.org.uk

Preface

There are trials as well as triumphs in the ministry of an ordinary pastor. Often it's the trials that are not mentioned. Ask a pastor who attends ministers' fraternals. Read a testimony of a pastor in a Christian magazine. For those ministers that are going through trials, I pray this book that recalls them honestly and factually will help and even comfort you. For members of a local church reading this book, I pray that you will pray for and support your pastor through his trials as well as through his triumphs. Remember that "If you want a better pastor then pray for the one you have!"

Here is a worthwhile quote from C.H.Spurgeon, the Pastor for 38 years of what became known as The Metropolitan Tabernacle in South London during the nineteenth century. He is affectionately known as the "Prince of Preachers":

"I know that, whenever God chooses a man for the ministry, and means to make him useful, if that man hopes to have an easy life of it, he will be the most disappointed mortal in the world. From the day when God calls him to be one of his captains, and says to him, 'See I have made thee to be a leader of the hosts of Israel,' he must accept all that his commission includes, even if that involves a sevenfold measure of abuse, misrepresentation, and slander. We need greater soul-exercise than any of our flock, or else we shall not keep ahead of them. We shall not be able to teach others unless God thus teaches us. We must have fellowship with Christ in suffering as well as fellowship in faith. Still, with all its drawbacks, it is a blessed service, and we would not retire from it. Did we not accept all this with our commission? Then we should be cowards and deserters if we were to turn back. These castings down of the spirit are part of our calling. If you are to be a good soldier of Jesus Christ, you must endure hardness. You will have to lie in the trenches, sometimes, with a bullet lodged here or there, with a sabre-cut on your

forehead, or an arm or a leg shot away; where there is war, there must be wounds, and there must be war where there is to be victory."

The ministry for me has felt like a battlefield. When we surrender our lives to the Lord Jesus Christ He takes us on as soldiers. *"You therefore must endure hardship as a good soldier of Jesus Christ. No one engaged in warfare entangles himself with the affairs of this life, that he may please him who enlisted him as a soldier,"* (2 Timothy 2:3,4). He is *"Commander of the army of the Lord"* (Joshua 5:14); He is the *"Captain of our salvation"* (Hebrews 2:10). There have been times of advance, when people have been blessed, but then comes a counterattack with the resultant losses. Sometimes there have been pre-emptive strikes, intended to halt or even reverse an advance. A victory may be immediately followed by a defeat, just as with Elijah when he challenged and defeated the prophets of Baal on the top of Mount Carmel. Within days his discouragement led him to ask God to take his life! I have often heard of pastors wanting to resign on Monday mornings. I have felt that way often too. We have shrapnel from passing through minefields of hardships; bullet wounds from ambushes of criticisms; setbacks from desertions under artillery bombardment; bayonet wounds from hand-to-hand combat with discouragement and betrayal. We do not command our troops from a safe distance. Rather we lead from the front and so often take the wounds intended for those we lead.

The very worst attack is what is called "blue on blue" or "friendly fire". When I taught biology to 18-year-olds as a school teacher in what was then Rhodesia I had in my class a particularly talented young man. He was highly intelligent, vice-captain of both the 1st Team Rugby and the 1st Team Cricket, and he was the Head Boy. His parents were former farmers. They were forced off their farm by intense terrorist activity in that part of Rhodesia, and now were teaching at the same school. They were immensely proud of their eldest son. On completion of his schooling William was conscripted into the Rhodesian Army. He was put through Officer Training and passed out as a 2nd Lieutenant. He was assigned to the Rhodesian African Rifles and one day led a platoon into battle with ZIPRA terrorists. In the ensuing fire-fight William was fatally shot – in the back. Forensics pointed to him being shot by his own men. That only aggravated the intense grief his parents and younger brother suffered.

Many of my own wounds in the ministry have been from members of my congregation, or worse still, from ministerial colleagues. These wounds have hurt the most. Praise the Lord that we have a Redeemer who not only redeems us from the curse of the law, but also from the bitterness of our stories. What's more, He redeems those stories too – by using them to help others with similar stories. With my stories I will also share the lessons I believe I may never have learned otherwise. You may draw your own lessons from these stories. There are possibly things you would have done differently if you were in my shoes.

Recently I rediscovered the prophecy given me at my ordination on April 11th 1982. It has proven very accurate and I include it here:

"As I lay hands upon you on your appointment as a pastor, *'the Lord bless you, the Lord lift up the light of His countenance upon you, and the Lord give you His peace.'* It is peace that you need for you are in a place of turmoil. Therefore My peace I give to you so you will know that whatever happens, yes, as you are in the centre of My will, you will rejoice because My will is always best. Know that you are in the school of the Holy Spirit. Therefore do not fret because of the hardness of the way because you are being schooled, says the Lord, for that which yet lies before you. Therefore take the schooling in a spirit of humility, of acceptance, and of rejoicing that you might be triumphant over all sets of circumstances in your own life, and the triumph in your life will bring blessings to others who need the same. Therefore be strong in the Lord, and go forward with Him for He is the One that desires to direct you from this day in an ever increasing way of blessings under His hand, even in the midst of trials and tribulation. Rejoice in the Lord."

When I wrote my first book Privileged Witness one of my proofreaders advised me to not include the story *My Dealings with an Alcoholic*. He felt that I should not include a story with so many setbacks. Or at least I should gloss over those setbacks. I had passed the story by my alcoholic friend who told me that I must include everything. He believed that it would go a long way to help people understand the addiction and possibly directly help others with similar addictions. I discussed this with my eldest son Mike. He said something very telling. "Setbacks are what you have had throughout your ministry, dad. Your readers must not be led to believe that it is easy to be a pastor. I know that it has not been."

Be Calm and Carry On was a wartime slogan. It described the "Stiff Upper Lip" attitude of our nation. You are to pick yourself up, dust yourself off, and carry on regardless. It seems to be an attitude especially expected of local pastors. Some pastors find that very hard to keep up. Hence the tragic fall-out from the ministry of very fine, and called, ministers. When I have shared my trials either at ministers' fraternals or with individual pastors, I have found a refreshing honesty as they open up about what has been going on beneath the surface in their lives and ministries. I do not include their stories in this book. It will be up to them to share those. These are my stories. All the names, including the name of my last church town, have been changed (except ours). One or more stories may resonate with my colleagues in ministry. When I told a colleague about this book he commented, "It must be a very big book!" He was not being sarcastic. He was telling me that he has found it hard too. I tell only a fraction of what could be told. I pray that God has led me in the writing of every story.

In every epistle of Paul he writes about his trials. One notable example is 2 Corinthians 1:8–11: *"For we do not want you to be ignorant, brethren, of our trouble which came to us in Asia: that we were burdened beyond measure, above strength, so that we despaired even of life. Yes, we had the sentence of death in ourselves, that we should not trust in ourselves but in God who raises the dead, who delivered us from so great a death, and does deliver us; in whom we trust that*

He will still deliver us, you also helping together in prayer for us, that thanks may be given by many persons on our behalf for the gift granted to us through many."

Sometimes Paul names and shames those who have wounded him. For example, in his personal letter to Timothy (2 Timothy 4:14,15) he writes; *"Alexander the coppersmith did me much harm. May the Lord repay him according to his works. You also must beware of him, for he has greatly resisted our words".* In a private letter to Gaius, the beloved apostle John writes, *"I wrote to the church, but Diotrephes, who loves to have the preeminence among them, does not receive us. Therefore, if I come, I will call to mind his deeds which he does, prating against us with malicious words. And not content with that, he himself does not receive the brethren, and forbids those who wish to, putting them out of the church. Beloved, do not imitate what is evil, but what is good. He who does good is of God, but he who does evil has not seen God. Demetrius has a good testimony from all, and from the truth itself. And we also bear witness, and you know that our testimony is true,"* (3 John:9–12).

God even lets us know the private conversations between Job and his friends Eliphaz the Temanite, Bildad the Shuhite, Zophar the Naamathite, and young Elihu the Buzite. We are also told the private conversations between our Lord Jesus and Simon Peter in Matthew 16:23; Luke 22:31–34; and John 21:15–22. He does this not to break confidence, but to authenticate the whole story and help His readers (1 Corinthians 10:11; 2 Timothy 3:16,17).

I was greatly encouraged to go ahead and publish this book after reading *Wounded by God's People*, an excellent book by Anne Graham-Lotz.

I have passed the contents by a CWR trained counsellor to see whether I "still have issues" that I have not yet worked through and resolved. I pray that if any of these stories raise issues with you, you will seek counsel, and receive God's grace and healing too.

✝CHAPTER 1

Lessons from Usurping Another

"The Executive have met and discussed the need for a pastor in our churches in Redcliff and Kwe Kwe," said Pastor Bob. He had called me into his office and closed the door behind us. I had the feeling that he was about to ask me something that would launch my ministry. It was September 1st, 1980 and I still had four months to go with my Bible College training. Back in January of that year I had requested that I complete my training by correspondence but my request had been turned down. The reason for that request was my wife Clare was pregnant with our first child and the baby was due in July. Clare had been working to support me through Bible College and she would need to stop work at least a month before the due date. I felt that I had the responsibility to provide for her and our child. "This is a golden opportunity for you to trust God with all your needs," Pastor Bob had told me back then. I simply accepted that instruction and went back to study as usual. In my book *Privileged Witness* I describe how wonderfully God met all our needs.

"We have unanimously decided to offer you the post of pastor of those churches. We know that you carry a burden for Zimbabwe and that you are prepared to return there even though it now has Mr Mugabe in power," Pastor Bob continued. He paused to gauge my reaction. I was struck dumb. I had never been to Redcliff before – it was a village off the main road and I had only ever passed through Kwe Kwe on the way to or from Harare, Zimbabwe's capital. Pastor Bob interrupted my racing thoughts with, "I will give you and Clare time to prayerfully consider this opportunity. However, we will need to know soon as the need there is desperate. If we cannot find anyone to go there soon we will be forced to close those churches down."

"We'll go!" I blurted out. Both Clare and I had agreed to go wherever God sent us, and although this would not have been our preferred first pastorate, it was a start. I felt honoured to have been asked to leave college early and to be given a pastorate of my own. I knew that the policy was for a Bible College trained person to first serve at least two years "apprenticeship" under an experienced minister before being entrusted with his own church.

"As you know, John, this is not normal procedure," said Pastor Bob. I felt that he had been reading my mind. "You will come under the supervision of Pastor Charles in Gweru. You will need to report to him at least once a month, and he will be on call anytime you may need him for wise counsel. As for your studies – we will expect you to complete them by correspondence and to write the final examinations in Gweru at the same time as your colleagues here at Bible College."

I asked him when I was expected to start and he told me "as soon as possible John! As you know, there is a wave of emigration from Zimbabwe and this is affecting the church there too. At present, the Kwe Kwe and Redcliff churches are being pastored by our missionary, Pastor Mark. He is struggling to hold the churches together, and being a bachelor does not help. We believe that you are up to the job and we'll be committed to praying for you and supporting you any way we can."

"Could I begin there on the 1st October?" I asked. "That will give us time to pack up home, organise where we will live, and ship our furniture to Zimbabwe. And while the furniture is in transit," I somewhat boldly added, "could we have a little holiday as we will not be getting a holiday this December now?" He agreed wholeheartedly to my request and I left the room in a daze. I went straight home to tell Clare the news. It took her by surprise and was sweetened by the prospect of a holiday. We had both been committed Christians for ten years. From the beginning of our courtship she'd known God's call on me for His ministry and she had supported me in every way in preparing for it. Now the door had been flung open and our adventure together would enter a new phase.

Pastor Mark lived in a small rented home in Redcliff. He was to move out on the 31st September and we were to move in on the 1st October. I had left Clare and our two month old son, Michael, with her parents in Bulawayo. The packing up of home, the holiday at the coast with friends who were themselves needy, and the very long journey with a newborn son had exhausted Clare. I was greeted in Redcliff by the elder Jim and his wife Mary – and by Pastor Mark. They showed me the home, and when the removals van arrived at midday, they helped me place our belongings in the rooms. That night we all ate together at Jim and Mary's home. The atmosphere was decidedly tense with Pastor Mark making it quite obvious that he was very put out, and unhappy.

We discussed the short history of the churches in Redcliff and Kwe Kwe. It had been founded by Pastor Charles from Gweru. He had been invited by Tony and Elaine, who had moved to Kwe Kwe from Gweru, to a small number of people that they had gathered in their home. Mary had been one of them, and she committed her life to Christ at that meeting. She then invited Jim to the next meeting. He reluctantly went. Tony had put out an offering box, and Mary persuaded her husband to put a substantial donation into it. After the sermon, Pastor Charles invited anyone with need to the front for prayer. Mary took her daughter Shirley forward, and she was prayed for with the laying on of hands. So confident was Mary that God had answered the prayer, that she gave Shirley a glass of milk to drink, and some dairy ice-cream to eat. She and her angered husband then watched to see whether Shirley would have any severe allergic reaction to dairy products as before. There were none. Shirley had been healed.

At the next meeting Jim surrendered himself to Jesus Christ. They told me that their chemist bill for Shirley's medication was more than the tithe they had put in the box that night! Pastor Donald (a bachelor) had then been called to pastor the church. He had set up a 6.30pm service at the Redcliff Anglian Church, and a meeting in a community hall in Kwe Kwe at 10.30am Sunday mornings. The church was growing until a crisis at our Mutare Church (the incumbent minister suddenly left for personal reasons) necessitated Pastor Donald moving there, to be replaced by his half-brother and missionary, Pastor Mark. Now Clare and I were replacing Pastor Mark, and he was clearly not happy about that. He left the next morning for Harare.

By the weekend the house was in order, I had met with Tony and Elaine, and some others, at the house-group in their home, and I had fetched Clare and Michael from Bulawayo. At our first Sunday meetings Jim led the worship with Elaine playing the keyboard. I preached. Elaine discovered that Clare could play keyboard, and she was quite prepared to have Clare play in her place. They then agreed, as both had young children, that they would share. Clare and I soon settled into our new roles with ease, and with much appreciation. More than once we were told how grateful they were to have a married pastor and not a bachelor. "The miracle with Pastor Mark," they told us, "was that though he fumbled and bumbled in relating to them personally, he was very fluent in his prayers and preaching." His half-brother Donald, by contrast, was very confident in every situation, and with everyone.

I tried to put myself in Pastor Mark's shoes. How would I feel if I was usurped by a much younger man who had been released from Bible College four months early to take my place? As far as I know, he was not given any reason for the change of pastor. He loved the people in the church. Emigration of church members would not stop after the change. God was blessing his prayers and preaching. The two things that he seemed to be judged on were his lack of confidence in relating individually with members, and his lack of a wife. Unfortunately his resentment showed, and I was ill-equipped to reverse that at the time. I was not even given the opportunity to have a farewell party for him, and to thank him for his ministry.

Two years later I felt very unsettled when Jim and Mary announced that they were leaving Redcliff to start a life in Johannesburg. He had been offered employment selling used cars from a car stand owned by a relative. When Tony, my other elder, announced that he was being promoted, and transferred back to Gweru, I fasted and prayed for direction from the Lord. I received a strong impression that God wanted me in Harare, Zimbabwe's capital. So I arranged to visit my mother there. I did not tell her my mission. From her home I phoned Pastor Sidney, asking him whether we could meet up. He told me that if I wanted to see him I would need to come first to his 6am prayer-meeting the next morning. He would see me straight after that. I went. After the prayer-meeting he began a conversation with one of his elders, and I waited around for long time. It became obvious that he had no interest in seeing me so I turned to Pastor Mark, and I asked him whether there were any plans to church-plant from the Belvedere Church. "Why are you asking me that?" he asked. I told him that I had a strong impression that God was calling me to minister in the capital, and I wondered whether there were any openings. Pastor Mark seemed indignant, and told me curtly to "stand in line – there were others ahead of you if there is to be a church-plant." I assumed he had put himself ahead of me too. His resentment toward me once again seemed obvious to me. I felt bad about it but this time I did not feel responsible for his issues. Neither did I want a repeat of what happened when I was appointed to take his place in Redcliff and Kwe Kwe. I asked him to excuse me from Pastor Sidney, and I returned to Redcliff.

When home I wrote a letter to our South African Headquarters General Secretary, Pastor Thomas. I told him of my leading, without mentioning my exploratory trip to Harare. I received a reply the following Thursday. He told me that there was absolutely no opening for me in Harare, and that if I felt it was time to move, I should consider a move to South Africa where they would be delighted to place me in a church needing a pastor. That Sunday afternoon my mother phoned me. She was distraught. "You will never believe what happened in church this morning, son! Pastor Sidney announced that he was leaving the denomination forthwith, and taking up the pastorate of an independent church in Harare. He encouraged the whole congregation to join him as he saw no future for any of us within the denomination. He is so popular here that I am sure the congregation will join him. I cannot believe it's happened. Please pray for us, son!" I could not have foreseen that happening. It deeply saddened, and yet gladdened me at the same time. My impression had been from the Lord who knows the end from the beginning.

That weekend I went to the annual Easter Convention in Pretoria, South Africa. Whilst there I was greeted by Pastor Thomas. "Do you know that Pastor Sidney has resigned, and left the denomination?" he asked. I told him that my mother had told me. "There will be no debate as to who to send to replace him, you know. I'll be showing your letter to the executive when we meet on Tuesday, and you'll hear from us soon afterwards." As he left me I heard him mutter "That was some leading of the Lord!"

Since Clare was not with me that convention (she was due any day with our second child, and I was there because that year I was ordained, having served two years probation), I remained after the Sunday evening service to pray silently for those who had gone forward for prayer. As he was closing, the convener looked around and noticed me. He called me and told me that he had scheduled Pastor Sidney to preach at the closing service of the convention. He then told me that Pastor Sidney had passport problems, and had to turn back at the Zimbabwe border. Could I take his place? I keenly felt the irony of this request. I said yes, and preached my first ever convention message. A few days after returning home our son Timothy was born. I was so grateful to be home for that too.

Within two weeks of that convention Pastor Bob fetched me to go with him to try and retrieve the situation in our Harare church. He had founded and built the church there, and was very keen to salvage what he could. Our first port of call was Pastor Sidney's house. Pastor Bob asked him his reasons for leaving the church and denomination. He showed Pastor Bob an interpretation of a "vision" someone had had for him. Pastor Bob read it and passed it on to me to read. Just as I was thinking "this is telling Pastor Sidney to stay", Pastor Bob said, "I believe that this vision and interpretation are telling you to stay, and not to leave."

Pastor Sidney replied, "Absolutely not – it is telling me to go, and that is what I am doing. I was warned you would try to persuade me to stay. There is nothing you can say that will persuade me otherwise." Pastor Bob expressed his sorrow at Pastor Sidney's decision, and offered to pray before we left. Pastor Sidney reluctantly agreed, and after a sincere prayer for God's blessing and guidance, we left. I told Pastor Bob in the car that for a moment I had thought I'd be going back to Redcliff! For the next couple of days he and I visited a number of members, trying to persuade them to remain with the church, and introducing myself as the new minister. That was truly grueling – I was well out of my comfort zone.

What was also difficult was serving notice on Pastor Mark to vacate the manse. When we met up with him he was persuaded by Pastor Bob to remain with the denomination. I honestly would have preferred it if he had joined with Pastor Sidney. I had usurped him again. Was there a lesson I had not learned first time around? Maybe there was a lesson God wanted to teach him? All my dealings with him in the first few months were unhappy. So I proposed that he went on a missionary tour of Zimbabwe – and despite our financial hardship, I agreed to fully sponsor the tour from church funds. He reluctantly agreed and off he went.

The end of Pastor Mark's tour coincided with our Annual Convention in Bulawayo. He told me that the Lord had greatly blessed his trip, and that many were saved and blessed through his ministry. I was delighted until I overheard him tell a colleague, "I cannot stand it being told by *that* John Henson what to do and where to go!" So I quoted him to Pastor Charles, asking him to transfer Pastor Mark to Gweru where he could take his orders from a minister who is his senior, rather than from me, who was his junior. Pastor Charles saw the wisdom in my request, and Pastor Mark went on to enjoy effective ministry under Pastor Charles. My relationship with him also improved, first because I was always respectful and encouraging to him, and secondly when he reciprocated. Twenty years later he chose to retire to a small village south of Hailsford, and make our church his spiritual home. He made me feel like his pastor and friend too! I remain so grateful to God for turning things around so graciously.

†CHAPTER 2

Lessons from Mentors

S oon after we had settled in Redcliff, Clare and I went through to Gweru to speak to our supervising minister, Pastor Charles and his wife Penny. The appointment was for 10.30am and we arrived in good time. Penny greeted us and apologised for Pastor Charles' absence. He had gone to town to bank the church money, and no doubt had been waylaid by someone he knew. "He is very well known in Gweru," added Penny. She ran a renowned crèche, and was excellent with the children. She showed us around her crèche, which was in an extension of their home, and then sat us down for tea and scones.

When Pastor Charles arrived he explained that he had met a couple of folk in town who had detained him. After asking whether we had settled in well, he proceeded to tell us his story. He had worked for Ford Motor Company in Fort Victoria in their spare-parts division. Then he was asked to pastor a church in Gweru, where there were a couple of families interested in forming a church. He told us how that he had been told to "burn his boats" and "trust the Lord for everything". There would be no help coming from his church back in Fort Victoria – or indeed from anywhere in the denomination. He was "on his own"! He explained that this was very hard, especially as the small congregation did not see any growth for month after month. He told us how hard it had been to put food on the table for Penny, and their two children.

The breakthrough came when he reached the end of himself and spoke angrily to God about his predicament. "When I worked for Ford I could provide adequately for my family. Now that I work for the church, I find that impossible. I should never have come here! I should never have opened this Bible!" Just then in the garden where he was sitting, a sudden wind blew the pages of his Bible, and then disappeared. He looked to where the pages had turned and read; *"You shall speak My words to them, whether they hear or whether they refuse, for they are rebellious. But you, son of man, hear what I say to you. Do not be rebellious like that rebellious house; open your mouth and eat what I give you,"* (Ezekiel 2:7,8).

Pastor Charles then described a conversation with the Lord. He felt the Lord ask him, "Whose church is this?"

He thought a while, and then said, "I suppose that it is Yours, Lord."

"Then let us keep it that way!" was the stern reply. "When you worked for Ford, who took full responsibility for the firm?"

"I suppose the General Manager!"

"And who did you turn to when problems arose?"

"The General Manager."

"Then that is how it must work with you and Me as you serve Me in My Church."

"Trusting God alone and obeying His orders from that day on was the reason for the steady growth and blessing of the church," Pastor Charles told us. "And let that be a lesson for you." He went on to tell us some amazing stories of salvations, healing and even deliverances that left us in awe. It took us a few more visits to realise that Pastor Charles and Penny were not going to mentor us at all. We were to trust and obey the Lord alone! Invariably our monthly visits found Pastor Charles late from town. When we did get down to talk he spoke about cars, his model-airplane hobby, his garden, and some of his stories. He changed the subject if we asked questions relating to difficulties we were experiencing as new ministers. In December of our first year I sat the exams that my fellow students at Bible College were sitting, and our visits to Gweru tailed off.

God was bringing new people into the church with a few conversions to Christ. Those were what meant the world to me, and I often feel that fruit, as in converts, are the victories on the battlefield of ministry. However, Zimbabwe was changing, and countless white Zimbabweans were emigrating, including from our little churches. We would have a visit from members who would question us about coming back to Zimbabwe after Bible College in South Africa. "Don't you know that Zimbabwe is now ruled by communist terrorists? Do you know what the communists do to Christians, and especially Christian pastors? You have a son, they could take him away from you..." They would also come with a long list of justifications for their hasty exit from the country of their birth. Education, law and order, and health services were usually on the top of the list. Very rarely I was told that God was leading them. South African businesses were actively recruiting artisans – they had set up a recruiting agency at a local hotel. So when I was told "that God had opened a door for them in South Africa", I was skeptical.

Sometimes I would say, "We have returned to Zimbabwe because we felt God's call back here. We know that He has Christians living under every regime in the world. What is more, we believe that materialism has done more to dampen Christian fervour than persecution ever has. We are sure God will look after us!"

I took this problem to Pastor Charles and was told that his church was also facing the same issue, and that, like him, I should not let it affect me. I then took it to my colleague, Pastor Brian, in Kadoma. He said, "Whatever you do John, do not try to persuade them to stay, or hold on to them. They will tear away from you anyway – and your relationship with them may be ruined. Keep open hands! In other words, let them know you respect them, and their decision. Then bless them as they leave. Open hands leaves them free to go, and free to return. The relationships remain intact. I can go to any one of the folk who have left my church when I travel to South Africa or wherever, and they will welcome me with open arms. Also, very importantly, God sees the open hands and can easily 'replace' those you have lost."

That lesson of having open hands has remained with me ever since. It has really helped, no matter the reason people have had for leaving the churches I have pastored. Some of those departures have deeply wounded me, especially when I am severely criticised and my ministry rubbished. I have had former members return, to be welcomed back with "open hands". I have also applied this lesson to volunteers in the church. I tell them when they volunteer that should they ever want or need a break they should feel no shame in asking for one. I have seen too many volunteers "burning out" and then leaving the church as a way of recovering, rather than simply cutting back on their involvement. They end up in another church (or mine if they were burnt out in another) sitting at the back, unwilling to volunteer for anything again. I have also learned the benefit of annually celebrating the work of the volunteers – mentioning each by name and thanking them specifically for their vital and appreciated contribution to church life. I praise those who are so busy in secular life that their only involvements are their presence on the Lord's Day, and their faithful financial contributions.

I regularly attended the local evangelical ministers' fraternal in Kwe Kwe which was a huge blessing to me. Gradually we became more honest about what was really happening in our churches, and our friendships blossomed. What meant most were the devotionals at our meetings – and the heartfelt prayers for one another and for each other's church. I played squash regularly with Pastor Steven.

In our second year I decided to hold an outreach in the Kwe Kwe High School main hall. I secured the 16mm film *The Cross and the Switchblade* and advertised the event. I felt confident that Pastor Charles would lend us his church's 16mm projector for the occasion.

He refused on the grounds that he only trusted himself to operate it properly. I told him that as part of my post-graduate teacher-training, I had learned how to operate a 16mm projector. I had regularly used one when I had taught for two years prior to attending Bible College. I promised to collect it on the day of showing, and return it the day after. He still refused. I felt perplexed. Shortly afterwards we held a fraternal, at which I told them my dilemma. Pastor Dave immediately offered his projector and we made the event a combined effort of the churches to reach out to the lost. I was learning that Pastor Charles was sticking to his original policy that I must not look to him for anything.

I do believe in mentoring not only new pastors, but all pastors. Over the years I have always joined Ministers' Fraternals at least for the mutual support that they offer, even if unintentionally. I formed close friendships with some of my colleagues along the way, and will forever be grateful for their input into my life and ministry. We would share stories, discuss difficulties, and pray for one another. Clare also formed good friendships with some of the wives of pastors. She needed to know what God expected of her as a pastor's wife. In discussing this with her friend Wendy's mother Barbara, she was told, "I asked God to show me what my role was. He told me very clearly that I was to love and support my husband in his role (he was a missionary of long standing), and raise my three children to love and serve the Lord Jesus Christ. My son has gone into the ministry and both my daughters have married pastors. It was only when my children left home that God graciously gave me a role in leading intercession groups, and in women's ministry." After her husband Pastor Bill went to be with the Lord in heaven, God granted her an international ministry with women.

After our sons left home the Lord granted Clare a counselling ministry, and every month she has had an appointment with a supervisor who has mentored her. In Hailsford Clare started a pastors' wives support group which was a great blessing. Pastors' wives often have a rougher time from the ministry than their husbands. One pastor's wife in Hailsford refused to even attend her husband's church because of being so badly wounded by the expectations placed on her especially by the women in that church. She was a very "arty" person, and her make-up and clothing had been heavily criticised!

I still regard my Bible College Principal, Pastor Bob, as a mentor. Whenever he has visited us we have had in-depth discussions and prayer on the ministry. We have gleaned so much wisdom and encouragement from him over the years for which we shall be forever grateful. He has been there for both of us whenever we have passed through deep waters in our journey. He has been a big promoter of my books *Privileged Witness*, and *The Humility of God*. He has believed in us, inviting us to preach in South Africa at big conferences as well as his own church, and he has always remembered our birthdays!

†CHAPTER 3

Lessons on Balance

One of the first things I did in Redcliff was to read through the New Testament in my King James Version and write in it some of the amplifications found in the Amplified Bible. When I got to 1 Peter 5:7,8, I believe I had an inspirational teaching encounter with the Lord that I have never forgotten. I read in the Amplified Bible, *"Be well balanced (temperate, sober of mind), be vigilant and cautious at all times; for that enemy of yours, the devil, roams around like a lion roaring [in fierce hunger], seeking someone to seize upon and devour."*

I then had a clear mental picture of me walking a tight-rope in a Big Top. I was holding tightly onto a long bar that enabled me to keep my balance. In the grandstands around the perimeter was an audience watching to see if I would keep my balance, and make the walk to the end. Underneath me was a prowling "fiercely hungry" lion, looking up at me and roaring, waiting for me to lose my balance so as to feast on me. The bar, that was so vital for my balance, I understood represented the Word of God. I prayed that God would enable me to always keep my balance. I wanted to be balanced in my teaching and preaching so that I would end up preaching *"the full counsel of God"*, and not some pet doctrine or doctrines. I wanted to have a good work/home balance. I wanted to have God's Word rule my whole life. I wanted to reach the safety of the platform at the end of the tightrope. I wanted to finish strong! Twenty-five years later I read Steve Farrar's excellent book *Finishing Strong*. That book inspired me to read *The Leadership Secrets of Billy Graham* by Harold Myra and Marshall Shelley. I highly recommend these books to every Christian, and especially every pastor. They not only inspire us to finish strong, they teach what ambushes come our way, and they teach us how to shore ourselves up to prevent defeat.

Shortly after that "revelation" I attended an interdenominational men's breakfast at a local hotel. The speaker was the head-teacher of the Redcliff Primary School. He was a Baptist Christian. During a great talk he said something that I have never forgotten. It tied in so well with my "revelation" about balance. He said, "Always remember that if you are not prepared to go fishing with your child now, you will have to go hunting for him later." From then on I endeavoured, within the financial restraints of the ministry, to "go fishing" with my children. As they passed through schooling and tertiary education I did my best to be at every swimming gala, athletics event, rugby match, school play, graduation ceremony and music gig, and pass-out parade. I also never failed to take my family on holiday every year.

Many years after the lesson God taught me on balance Clare and I attended a "Marriage Enrichment Weekend". It was long after we had befriended Grant and Sarah. Grant was a professor of mathematics at the University of Zimbabwe and his wife Sarah was the head of the English Department at a private girls' secondary school. We had known them for years. They lived in a northern suburb of Harare near the university. They attended a thriving church nearby, and they ran a house-group in their home. Most of the members of that group were themselves academics. When visiting them one day, we told them of our need for fellowship outside of our church family, and they generously invited us to join their house group. We loved it and thrived there.

Later on an American couple, Glen and Amy, joined that group. Glen was working at the university on a two year contract as a lecturer in philosophy. After about a year Glen and Amy were asked by Scripture Union to speak at a Marriage Enrichment weekend at a hotel on Fothergill Island on Lake Kariba. On hearing that, Clare and I immediately planned to go too. So I sold my .22 rifle to raise the money needed and we made the long journey north to Lake Kariba. About twenty married couples had booked to attend, including Grant and Sarah, who had come in our car with us.

We will never forget what God taught us there through this humble and committed couple. At the very first "lecture", Glen opened with, "I want you all to know that I live daily *in fear* for my marriage." He paused for a while as he surveyed his audience. Then he said, "I can see that many of you are shocked by what I have just said. Let me elaborate. All my life my father has been a pastor. I was raised in the church. Yet I have witnessed the break-up of many marriages that I thought were rock-solid. I am talking about the break-up of Christian marriages. That has made me ask the question, 'Who do I think Amy and I are, that given the same temptations, the same pressures, and the same circumstances, our marriage is safe?'" Then he introduced a new word when he continued, "So this *healthy* fear that we have for our marriage makes us every day work at it. We do not take anything for granted. This," he said with a sigh, "is the reason we have a truly happy marriage!" He then expounded on all the things that they worked at, and all the things that they did not take for granted. Over the weekend Glen and Amy were very honest with us all, and we came away refreshed in our marriage.

On the way home we discussed Glen's opening statement, and then we applied it to other issues. For example, we recalled how that in Philippians 2:12,13 we read: *"Therefore, my beloved, as you have always obeyed, not as in my presence only, but now much more in my absence, work out your own salvation with fear and trembling; for it is God who works in you both to will and to do for His good pleasure."*

We all knew fine Christians who have walked away from their Saviour. It may have begun with neglect of prayer, Bible study, or church fellowship. It may have been through falling for some temptation or temptations. Perhaps they were wounded by other Christians, or even their church leadership. Now who do we think we are that, given the same temptations, the same pressures, and the same circumstances, our relationship with Christ is safe? A *healthy* fear that we have for our salvation makes us every day work at it (in co-operation with God who *"works in us both to will and to do for His good pleasure"*). We do not take anything for granted. We will not neglect private prayer, Bible study, church fellowship or any other "means of grace". This will be the reason for us having a truly close walk with God!

Then we discussed how that we knew of many children of Christians, including "preachers' kids" who had rebelled and walked away from their Saviour, and their home values. Who do we think we are that, given the same temptations, the same pressures, and the same circumstances, our children's relationship with Christ, or with us, is safe? A *healthy* fear that we have for their walk with God makes us every day work at it. We do not take anything for granted. To this day, before we go to sleep at night, Clare and I hold hands and pray earnestly for our three sons. On and off through their growing years we have prayed for their future wives, believing that somewhere they are growing up too. We were thrilled to meet each one for the first time. And now we are overjoyed to be praying for our grandchildren, and occasionally their future spouses.

Many years later, and just before our eldest son Mike married Gem, we experienced in our Hailsford church the trauma of the divorce of Phil and Joy. I tell the story later in this book. What was so sad was to see how badly Phil's parents took this break-up. His father Mervyn had been "boasting" to me about all three of his children only weeks before the tragic split. He and his wife Kerry were thrilled at how their two daughters and Phil loved and served the Lord, and how they had each married godly spouses. It made Clare and I aware that we could never take it for granted that, given the same temptations, the same circumstances and the same pressures, our marriage and our sons' marriages will be "safe". So we pray for them every day without fail, and we are there for them should they ever ask for advice or help.

✝ CHAPTER 4

Lessons on the Power of Turning the Other Cheek

After a year in Redcliff a man called Kevin attended one of our meetings. A week later he phoned me, and asked to see me at his auto-spares shop. There he gave me an envelope with money in it. He told me that God had told him to pay his tithe to my church. Not being able to argue with "God told me," I accepted. I should have asked more questions – like "Why?" I admit I did not even ask God as to whether or not I should accept it. Little did I know I was to face the biggest trial of my ministry to date. The next month Kevin came back to church, now with his demure wife Julia. After the service he told me how much he appreciated the fact that I knew the Word of God so well. He then announced that God had told him to become a part of our church. This time I asked him about his previous church history. He had been in Pastor Dan's church. There had been some misunderstandings there and he felt it was now time to move on.

At the next fraternal I asked Pastor Dan about Kevin and Julia. I was told that there had been misunderstandings, and that it would be better for them to move to us. It would be hard for Julia as she had very good friendships in his church – but she was a "good submissive wife" who would do as Kevin wished. I failed to even wonder why

Pastor Dan did not mention Kevin having friends in his church, let alone ask about this anomaly. Pastor Dan had failed to tell me the whole truth.

At a home visit Kevin told me his spiritual giftings. He had been a Christian for about thirty years. During that time he had been an elder, and his preaching ministry was sought after. He ran his own successful business, and tithed to the penny. When at school he had been a first team rugby player and chief try-scorer. He had been high up in many jobs before venturing out with a business of his own. I discovered that Julia was a very quiet "background" intercessor. I sensed she had a very sincere and deep relationship with the Lord Jesus, and my heart really warmed towards her.

I had previously trained my elders, Tony and Jim, to preach. I had given both of them opportunities to preach in services as I appraised them. Both of them had told me how many hours it had taken them to prepare their twenty minute sermons (up to fourteen hours), and both of them told me how much they admired me for preparing three sermons for each Sunday and one Bible Study each mid-week. So when I was going on holiday, and missing four Sundays, I decided to give them each one Sunday to do, including Kevin (whom I had not heard preach yet, I am ashamed to say). That left one Sunday that needed a preacher. I knew an elder in the Gweru church who was a good preacher, and I asked him to cover the last Sunday.

When I first met Tony after returning from holiday he told me how angry Kevin had been that I had asked an elder from Gweru to take the last Sunday services. "Could John not trust us to cover that Sunday too?" he had argued. Tony was trying to warn me of the reception I could expect when I next saw Kevin. After service the next Sunday I took Kevin aside to explain my decision. I told him that I had heard that he was not happy about me calling an elder from Gweru to take a Sunday's services. Before I could reason that I knew that sermon-preparation takes long hours, he demanded to know who had told me that he was angry (not the word I had used).

I told him it was Tony, and then I tried to explain my reasons. I sensed he was not listening, and I felt guilty "for having blown it".

I was not surprised to receive a phone call the next day from Kevin. He asked to see me as soon as possible at his shop. As it was my day off with my family, I told him I'd be there at 10am on Tuesday.

Kevin did not greet me as I entered his shop. He stood behind the wooden counter, and I stopped near the door, diagonally opposite him. "You know what the Bible says!" he began, and then paused for my reply.

"Yes," I tentatively replied, not knowing what part of the Bible he was referring to.

"*If your brother sins against you, go and tell him his fault between you and him alone,*" he said assertively.

"Yes," I said again, just as tentatively.

"Then the Bible goes on to say '*But if he will not hear, take with you one or two more, that by the mouth of two or three witnesses every word may be established.*'" Again he waited for me to acknowledge him.

I replied "yes", still not knowing what he was leading up to.

"I know that Tony will not hear me if I went to him alone, so I am taking the next step, and asking you to come to see him as my witness!"

His tone of voice made me realise that he was not requesting but demanding. Under my breath I called on the Lord for His wisdom. Then with a confidence and authority that was not my own, I said, "No, I will not!"

"Why not?" he ranted.

"Because the first verse you quoted ends with '*If he hears you, you have gained your brother*'. I believe you do not want to confront Tony in order to *gain him*, but in order to humiliate him – and I will have no part in that!"

"I thought that there were only two people in Kwe Kwe and Redcliff who heard from God, now I know that there is only one!" he ranted, the veins of his neck standing proud and his face turning red.

I then had a vivid image in my mind of him reaching to a shelf under his counter for a large lump of mud. I sensed he had pre-prepared this should I not comply with his demands. He lifted this "lump" onto the counter, and he grabbed a handful to throw at me. It was a stinging criticism of my youth and inexperience as a pastor. Who was I to say "No" to him when he heard so clearly from the Lord?

I called on God again for what to do now, and the verse came clear to my mind *"turn the other cheek"*. I seemed to intuitively know what that meant in this pressured situation. I straightened my shoulders, and looked him straight in the eye without flinching. Then a most amazing thing happened. I felt the pressure to react lift off me, and pass back onto him. This seemed to enrage him, and he grabbed another fistful of mud, and hurled it at me. It was a more stinging criticism, this time on my character, and identity. I cannot say that it did not hurt. Nevertheless I remained calm, still looking him straight in the eye. Again I felt the pressure to react lift off me, and return to him. I also sensed that if I had retaliated I would only be adding to his pile of mud. He then grabbed one fistful after another in a frenzy to get a reaction from me. I was awestruck at the power of turning the other cheek – and I was delighted to see the pile of mud reduce to nothing.

Kevin was the one who had "lost it", and he showed signs of exhaustion from the effort. He mumbled some things about having had a hard time lately, and that perhaps he should not have said some of the things he did. He then told me that I had better go, and that he was finished with me. I left in solemn silence, sensing that his embarrassment meant that he would no longer be coming to our fellowship. I felt especially sad for Julia who had made new friends, and who was so well loved by us all.

To my horror Kevin was not finished with me yet. In the week that followed, and at church the following Sunday, I was told by members of our two fellowships that Kevin had been slandering me, and actively trying to persuade folk to leave our church.

I brought the matter to our fraternal, and to my surprise, Pastor Dan's eyes filled with tears. "Oh, John, I am so sorry! Please forgive me! I should have told you about the so-called 'misunderstandings' we had with Kevin which made him leave us for you. He's doing the same with you as he did to me. I should have warned you, and protected you! I believe now that yours is the seventh church he has sought to break up."

I was very grateful for the prayers that were offered by my colleagues, and friends, that day! And I was very grateful to God that the whole congregation rallied around me to affirm me. No one except Kevin and Julia left us. Years later I learned from Oswald Smith in his wonderful book *Passion for Souls* that the best strategy when faced with personal criticisms is to have the principle of "No defence and no attack". In other words, do not give your "enemies" any more ammunition to use against you. Turn the other cheek and they will soon exhaust and betray themselves. Allow God the privilege to vindicate you – and to change you if any of the "mud" sticks.

✝CHAPTER 5

Life-time Lessons on Forgiveness

In the aftermath of Kevin and Julia's departure I went into a very dark time. I remember well one day when I felt especially low. I was alone in my little office. I got down on my knees to pray, and then stood up again as I proclaimed, "It is no use to pray! God has left me! A year and a half into my ministry and everything is unravelling. I have failed, I have failed!"

I had withdrawn from Clare and our son Michael. Her constant assurances that she, God, and the congregations loved me, affirmed me, and remained loyal, did not lift my spirits. I felt that the One that mattered most to me had forsaken me. I felt my prayers were hitting the ceiling, and bouncing back. I was morose, and I knew I had to break from that!

In the quietness of the room God reminded me of Hebrews 13:5,6. I had memorised those verses eleven years before but now I knew them in the Amplified version. Here they are: *"Let your character or moral disposition be free from love of money [including greed, avarice, lust, and craving for earthly possessions] and be satisfied with your present [circumstances and with what you have]; for He [God] Himself has said, I will not in any way fail you nor give you up nor leave you without support. [I will] not, [I will] not, [I will] not in any degree leave* you helpless nor forsake nor let [you] down (relax My hold on you)! [Assuredly not!] So we take comfort and are encouraged and confidently and boldly say, The Lord is my Helper; I will not be seized with alarm [I will not fear or dread or be terrified]. What can man do to me?"

This may seem ridiculous now, but I wrestled with that verse for what seemed like ages. The breakthrough came when God was gracious to me and let me *feel* His presence. He had never left me – and He never will!

I came out of the room quite different. Without me saying a word, Clare knew that God had answered her prayers, and met with me.

I wish that I could tell you that from that day I walked in victory. Not so! I became obsessed with Kevin and the damage he had brought to Christ's church. I sincerely wanted God to do to him what He had done to Ananias and Sapphira in Acts 5. I had been a passenger in his van once, and he had complained that his tie-rod ends were worn and needed to be replaced. So I suggested to God that He cause them to snap as he rounded a sharp bend at speed. I shudder now at how murderous I was then. I admit I was young and immature. Perhaps some of Kevin's criticism of me stuck.

After days of advising God, instructing God and trying hard to persuade God, I heard His still small voice speaking to me. I have very seldom heard "words" like that. Normally God has spoken though the written word of His Bible as He did when reminding me of the verse to *"turn the other cheek"*, and Hebrews 13:5,6. Other times I have felt a knowing – perhaps an intuition, leaning, pull or burden. But this time I felt I heard the words, and they arrested me. "Get out of My way" were the words I heard. They came to me quite out of the blue, when I was least expecting them, and I felt His presence as I heard them. I then questioned myself as to what the words meant. I reasoned that God wanted to handle Kevin without my advice or instruction. I remembered how that in Romans 12:19 God says, *"Beloved, never avenge yourselves, but leave the way open for [God's] wrath; for it is written, Vengeance is Mine, I will repay (requite), says the Lord."*

I told the Lord that I was very sorry for my pride in telling Him what to do. Kevin's sin was primarily against the Lord, and who was I to take it personally? I remembered then how the Lord Jesus had confronted Saul of Tarsus with these words: *"Saul, Saul, why are you persecuting Me [harassing, troubling, and molesting Me]?" And Saul said, "Who are You, Lord?" And He said, "I am Jesus, Whom you are persecuting. It is dangerous and it will turn out badly for you to keep kicking against the goad [to offer vain and perilous resistance],"* (Acts 9:5).

History recorded that Saul was persecuting the church – yet the Lord Jesus was taking that personally! King David had sinned against his wives, his children, Bathsheba, Uriah, and his nation, yet he knew his greatest sin was against Almighty God. He wrote, *"Against You, You only, have I sinned, and done this evil in Your sight – That You may be found just when You speak, and blameless when You judge,"* (Psalm 51:4).

A sin against a fellow human being is a violation of God's law to love, and therefore is primarily a sin against God. In personal cases like mine with Kevin, I was to allow God to handle the matter His way, and in His time. He is the only one who knows all the facts of the case, and He is the only one who is truly just. I knew that when there is a breaking of the laws of the land, I had every right to lay charges through the civil authorities. What Kevin was doing broke no civil law. It broke God's law, and therefore he had to answer to God, and not to me, or to society. I know that all this is common-sense, but I was learning it all as if it was fresh to me.

Then came another revelation that has helped me with forgiving others ever since. I remembered 1John 2:1,2 which reads: *"And if anyone sins, we have an Advocate with the Father, Jesus Christ the righteous. And He Himself is the propitiation for our sins, and not for ours only but also for the whole world."*

The Biblical definition of Advocate (Greek: *parakletos*), is "one who pleads another's cause, who helps another by defending or comforting him". It is a name given by Christ three times, to the Holy Spirit (John

14:16; 15:26; 16:7, where the Greek word is rendered "Comforter"). It is applied to Christ in 1 John 2:1, where the same Greek word is rendered "Advocate". Jesus Christ, who was the propitiation for all sin, was my Advocate with the Father. He would defend and comfort me and He would prosecute Kevin if He felt there was a case to be answered. He is the expert. He knows what He is doing. He'll do a far better job than I could ever do. If I would only put Kevin fully into His hands, He would handle everything on my behalf. I remembered the acrostic for faith – Father-All-In-Thy-Hands.

It was crazy the way I was handling things. It was as though I was holding a long charge sheet to Kevin's back, and not letting go. It seemed as though every time I began to pray I felt the need to pray "against" Kevin. He seemed to occupy far too much of my mind, and anger towards him occupied far too much of my heart. At night I dreamt about him. He occupied my waking thoughts, my thoughts throughout the day, and my thoughts before sleep overwhelmed me at night. If I saw him driving past, I would look away – and so would he! Now God was showing me the road to freedom. I was to "get out of His way" by handing the charge sheet to Him, and trusting my Advocate entirely with Kevin, and his sin.

It then dawned on me that Kevin was not the only one in my life that I needed to forgive. My life had been littered with offences, and my heart was full of wounds. Kevin was not the only one I never wanted to talk to again. If I was ever to be free, and if I was ever to *"become all things to all men, that I might by all means save some,"* (1Corinthians 9:22), I needed to forgive them all. I left my office to find Clare. I told her to please not allow anything to disturb me as I was wanting to stay in my office until I had completed "doing business with God". I returned to my office, closed the door behind me, and fell to my knees by my chair. I had been told that men's brains are like "filing cabinets", and that we can place memories into files which we then can put in order in the cabinet – with the bad memories' files "somewhere at the back".

My first prayer was asking the Lord to help me recall, and then deal with all the bad memories of my past. I was then amazed at how vividly I recalled the wounding of my heart – right back to early childhood, through those boarding-school days, through the years at university, through my years as a teacher and police-reservist, during my Bible College training and during my first year of ministry. I was looking at the "charge-sheet" for each person and then handing it over entirely to my Advocate. I was feeling the burden lifting with each forgiveness. The experience was becoming exhilarating. I forgave Pastor Charles for being so dismissive of my concerns in my new life as pastor.

Then I announced to the Lord, "Now for the big one – my current wounds! Lord, I forgive Kevin for all the criticism and slander he has levelled against me. I forgive him for all his endeavours to discredit me and the ministry You have called me to. I forgive him for his concerted efforts to break up our church. I give to You the charge sheet that I have held against him. I am getting out of Your way Lord, as You instructed me. Now the matter is between You and him alone. Please help me not to get involved in this case again."

Just then I was overwhelmed with compassion for Kevin. What if God took vengeance on him there and then? He was a poor lost soul. He was in a one man business because he always fell out with managers, and fellow-workers. He was so insecure. I felt all choked up and tears began to flow freely. I asked God to show him mercy, and to bless him with His full salvation. Just then my study seemed to fill with God's tangible presence. I pushed my chair away from me, and lay flat on my face before His holiness, and His comfort. As I write this, tears flow freely as I recall His awesome presence. I could not open my eyes lest I saw Him. I could not say a word. I truly revered Him! I felt wave upon wave of His matchless love caress my prostrate body. Words cannot describe how I felt.

I cannot say how long I lay there. The heaviness of God's presence lifted, I opened my eyes, lifted my head and looked around. As I stood on my feet I felt truly free. Jesus' words *"Therefore if the Son makes you free, you shall be free indeed"* (John 8:36), took on a whole new meaning. I felt real joy deep down in my heart. The pain had gone. I was healed. Praise His wonderful name! Before I opened the door of my office to go tell Clare my good news, I asked God that He would use me, and my experience, to bring the joy and freedom of forgiveness to other hurting people.

So what became of Kevin? He emigrated from Zimbabwe to live in South Africa. So did my trusted elder Jim. A couple of months later I received a letter from Jim. "You will never guess who pitched up at church last Sunday, John," he wrote. "Kevin and Julia! When the altar call was given at the end of the sermon Kevin was the first to respond. He was overcome with emotion, and stood in front crying his eyes out! After the service Mary and I went up to greet him and Julia. He told me this incredible story, and asked me to relay it to you. He had left Zimbabwe because he was a rabid racist – he hated the "blacks", and could not tolerate being ruled by them. He tried in vain to get a job with a white employer here in South Africa. Eventually when he was at the end of his resources, and the end of his tether, he took a job working for a black employer. He discovered that his employer had great business acumen, great values, and was every bit a human being as himself. He had gone to the front at the altar call to repent of his pride and prejudice! And John, God met with him, and he is a changed man! I am sure you will be delighted at this news!"

I was! In fact, I was so very glad that God has not taken my murderous advice, and that He had dealt so graciously with Kevin.

The lessons in forgiveness that I learned through my ordeal with Kevin I have applied and taught throughout my life as a pastor. They are, perhaps more than any other lessons, responsible for keeping me in the ministry. They prepared me for the battlefield ahead, where not only was I wounded by not-yet-Christians, but by Christians, and worse than that – by my colleagues and leaders within the church of Jesus Christ who shot me in the back in so-called "friendly fire".

I once shared Kevin's story during a sermon on *How to Forgive*. Rebecca was in our church for the first time. Although I had said in my sermon that some wounding was so severe that counselling was required to see the wounded through to healing, Rebecca still accused me of making forgiveness sound too easy. It was obvious that her wounding was very severe so I said to her, "I cannot help you with forgiveness Rebecca, but I know who can." I then introduced her to Clare who took her on as a client. Years later when Rebecca said farewell to our church to return to Kent, England, she testified to the church to being raped repeatedly by a close relative from an early age until she was able to escape to university. She said that if there was only one reason why God had brought her to our church, it was that He might heal her wounded heart through counselling. Jesus Christ and the Holy Spirit are truly wonderful counsellors! Rebecca sang a beautiful song giving God all the glory for her freedom in Christ. She then told us of her complete forgiveness of her relative, and that she is even communicating with him again! She then highly recommended counselling to anyone with a similar background. Clare thanked Rebecca for being a model client, having worked so hard with the process that ended with such liberty. Now Rebecca is equipped by God to help others with similar need.

†CHAPTER 6

Preaching Lessons

I decided in the second month of our ministry to teach my elders Jim and Tony how to preach. This was for when I was on holiday, at conference over a weekend, preaching elsewhere, or sick. I had received excellent training at Bible College and so I used my Homiletics notes. I taught them that the goal of all preaching was to change lives. *"Him we preach, warning every man and teaching every man in all wisdom, that we may present every man perfect in Christ Jesus. To this end I also labour, striving according to His working which works in me mightily,"* (Colossians 1:28,29).

It was never just to inform. Every sermon must have a clear theme running throughout so that the congregation knows, in one concise sentence, what was preached. The conclusion should be prepared first so that one has a clear goal. Then they were to prepare the body of the sermon, preferably in three or at most four sections or points. The use of alliterations would greatly aid memory both for the preacher and the listener. The sermon must begin with explanation and argument, and move on to persuasion and appeal. In other words, follow the pattern of New Testament Epistles and have the theology before the practical application.

The points must have harmonious relatedness and sequential

thrust. The sermon also needs relevant and contemporary illustrations as they are the windows that shed light on the sermon. Humour is good if appropriate, but must never be insensitive (at your wife's, children's, congregant's expense), sarcastic or coarse. Remembering that the congregation members cannot answer back during the sermon, it must never knowingly address specific issues or grievances in members. Sermons need to be reverent, respectful, and passionate too. Finally they need to construct the introduction which will introduce the theme and the points. The introduction tells the congregation what you will tell them in the body of the sermon, and the conclusion wraps it all up as you tell the congregation what you have just told them (in the body of the sermon).

Throughout the sermon the preacher needs to maintain connection with the congregation through eye contact. It can tell whether their listeners are receiving God's message, and they can tell when it is time to wind up the sermon. I taught them about gestures too. Some re-enforce the sermon, others distract the listeners. I warned them that the average time an adult can concentrate on a monologue was twenty minutes unless we "vary the stimuli" throughout the sermon. I emphasised the overriding importance of much prayer over every sermon. Only sermons inspired by the Holy Spirit can change lives.

After the lessons Jim and Tony had to prepare and preach a ten minute sermon for me to mark. That was quite an ordeal for them, but not as much as when I had them deliver their first sermon to the church. Tony told me how his respect for me and other preachers had increased dramatically. "It took me fourteen hours to prepare that twenty-minute sermon – I do not know how you come up with three sermons a Sunday, plus a Bible Study in the week!" he told me. Both elders equipped themselves well and that gave me both joy and confidence in them.

In my first year of ministry I journeyed down to Pretoria in South Africa to attend a seminar where Pastor Ed Roebert was the main speaker. I was struck by his humility and by his take on prosperity. He told us that when he was at Bible College both the lecturers and his peers made it clear that they did not believe he would ever make a preacher, let alone pastor a church. The diaconate of the Hatfield Baptist Church which reluctantly took him on after he graduated, told him that his post was temporary as they were looking for a "proper pastor".

When God graciously baptised Pastor Roebert with the Holy Spirit his ministry took off, and the church grew to being one of the largest in South Africa – despite him. On prosperity he said that he wanted to live simply and put other men into ministry with any extra money that God provided. It was his teaching on preaching however that made the biggest impact on me. He told us that when he announced to his father that he planned to go to Bible College to train for the ministry, his father made him promise that he would be a preacher of Good News. "The Gospel means 'Good News', son," he said with emotion. "Whenever I go to church the preacher makes me feel worse for his preaching. Don't do that to your congregation, son!" Pastor Ed was living proof of the power of preaching a positive message. That was a life-changing lesson for me for which I will always be grateful.

Another preaching lesson came from Dr Robert Coleman, an associate preacher with the Billy Graham Association. He preached in Harare in 1983, near the beginning of my ministry there. I still vividly remember his sermon! He preached that, "The Gospel comes in the Person of the Lord Jesus Christ! He is the Gospel! He is the Good News!" Ever since then I have endeavoured, by God's grace, to preach Jesus Christ, and Him crucified. In as far as religion means "way of life", I am happy to say Christianity is a religion. However I much prefer to call Christianity a relationship, secured by the substitutionary death of our one and only Saviour Jesus Christ.

The preachers I most admired during my early Christian life

were my first pastor when I was at university, and my Bible College Principal. Their concern was never only for the sheep in the fold. They were always keen on reaching the lost sheep. Throughout my ministry I have sought to learn the lessons they taught me. So, as with them, I give an altar call for sinners to meet their Saviour whenever I sense there are not-yet-Christians in the congregation. I learned at Bible College from the Betty Maltz story that "the only thing you can take to heaven is people – the rest you leave behind!" I have become obsessed that no one can say on Judgement Day that they went to my church and were never told *how* to repent and trust their Saviour to save them from hell.

In Hailsford I told a visiting preacher that we expected visitors at every service, and therefore I wanted him to preach sometime during his sermon the Gospel of Salvation and to give an altar call at the close of his sermon. At that service my middle son Tim and his friend had brought their not-yet-Christian colleague. He responded to the altar call and was soundly saved by God's grace – to the sheer surprise and delight of the guest preacher. To my horror, when that preacher returned to preach a year later his whole sermon was devoted to denouncing the preaching of salvation messages in church. Such messages, he dogmatically declared, were for the market-place and our neighbourhoods. The church was for church members only. He also denounced the use of a tithe box at the entrance of the church, saying that an offering bag should be passed around during the singing as an act of worship. He knew that I had the box to avoid expecting new-comers, and especially not-yet-Christians to contribute financially. I dare say that I never invited him back to preach again.

I need to also tell you about the lessons learned through my radio ministry. I had become very concerned that the preachers on our national radio station were "liberal" or "social Gospel" in their theology. I broached my concern at our evangelical Ministers' Fraternal. I asked them to join me to "squeeze out" those radio preachers by volunteering to preach on radio. No one joined me.

So I phoned Feba Radio who ran the 10.00am five minute slots five days a week. They were delighted to have on board another evangelical minister. On their recommendation I was invited by the Zimbabwe Broadcasting Corporation (ZBC) to preach at their noon five minute slot, and for a half hour on either their Sunday morning or Sunday evening slot.

It was at first very daunting to know that perhaps thousands of people would be listening to me. I had to type out the sermon in narrow columns and with double spacing. I had to deliver a copy of the sermon to the sound engineer. If I hesitated or made a mistake he would tell me where to begin again. I had been speaking for about a month when the ZBC offered a course on radio preaching. The lecturer was a very fine Christian and this is what he told us:

"If you are *not* going to preach the Gospel as found in the Bible, please do not preach at all! We also do not want you to mix the Gospel with ancestral-spirit worship or any other aberration." That really impressed me! Then he went on to give us this vital advice: "Remember that when you preach on radio you are speaking to only one person – that is the woman who is listening to the radio whilst she is ironing clothes, or the sick person as they are lying in a hospital bed, or the man who is driving his car and listening to the radio." From then on I pictured myself sitting down with one person – be it at their bedside, or in a car beside them as they drove, or on a sofa besides them in their home. Every message I preached on radio was specifically aimed to introduce our Saviour to sinners in need of His saving grace! I had very little feedback. I prayed the Holy Spirit would reach a lost and hurting Zimbabwe population through those messages. Heaven will tell if He did.

His advice also affected the way I preached at church. I became delighted when at least one person would tell me that the message was "tailor-made for me". God remains "the God of the individual"! It is noteworthy that at my farewells from Redcliff, Harare and Hailsford very little was mentioned on my preaching. What people thanked me for was my care and concern as demonstrated in "always being there for them", and specific ministry to them when they faced a crisis or drama. And of course there were grateful hearts for leading them to a personal relationship with Jesus Christ. I took solace in the fact that so many came faithfully week by week to worship and to hear God's Word preached.

I also learned a great lesson in preaching when playing golf one day with Pastor Bob. Knowing how well he played any ball game, I felt intimidated as I teed up for the first hole. I was sure that I would slice the ball into the rough, and that I would hold up his game by looking for my ball there. So I tensed up. As a result I did slice the ball into the rough.

"I notice how tense you are John!" Pastor Bob exclaimed. "Don't you know that you need to be relaxed if you want to hit a decent shot? Take another ball, and this time relax. I will give you one shot per hole as my handicap. Relax now and enjoy the game!"

I teed up again, took a deep breath, and relaxed. It was a perfect shot down the middle of the fairway! I was delighted. I went on to play the best golf to date. Pastor Bob then told me how that a relaxed delivery of a sermon was far more likely to hold the attention of a congregation. Instead of being distracted by the tension in the preacher, the congregation listens to the message itself. That advice (and the advice to practice before delivery) has helped me enormously with my preaching too.

I have found from my very first sermon until now, that I will always be tested on whether I practice what I preach or not. When I do, I have an authority: if I do not I lose authority (Matthew 7:27,28). Here is an example from Harare: I was delighted to have a church office. The manse was just yards away so I was near enough for Clare to call me when she needed me. The manse became a target for the beggars of Harare with their tales of woe. As we had very little money we had to turn most away. Some turned vicious when their pleas were unrewarded, so I determined that Clare was not to speak to them.

If I was away on a visit Clare told them to return later. Within a month we had our first burglary. I had read during a sermon *"Take heed and beware of covetousness, for one's life does not consist in the abundance of the things he possesses,"* (Luke 12:15) and I had commented that we know when possessions possess us when we are asked to give them away or they are taken from us – and we go to pieces.

I happened to go into the church for my jacket on the Monday morning to find that my jacket, and all the church carpets, were gone. We were not insured, so who knows when we could replace them. I went to pieces. It was going to ruin my day off with Clare and our sons. I had a sore head for most of the day – until I was reminded about the "possessions" challenge I had made the previous day. I fell to my knees asking God for forgiveness. I had failed the test. When I had peace I asked God for the recovery of the carpets. I did not want my jacket back. Just then I remembered that Pastor Sidney's house worker was the leader of the Zanu-PF youth league that patrolled the streets at night, looking after the community. I went there and asked for his help in tracking down the burglar. Within an hour he phoned me saying he had the burglar's name and address. I called the police and they arrested him. He had been the church warden, who mowed our lawns, cleaned our church and so on. I had to release him from service because of the church debt. He had rewarded me by raiding our church. We retrieved all our carpets and I re-laid them as before!

I learned a great lesson when I was still at university. I had studied for a Science Degree. Since there was often debate about science and the Bible, I especially read up creation research literature so that I could argue for the Bible accounts of creation, the flood and other such matters. These arguments sometimes became heated, with my "opponent" loading his "gun" whilst I spoke, and me loading mine whilst he spoke.

Then I read in 2 Timothy 2:24–26; *"A servant of the Lord must not quarrel but be gentle to all, able to teach, patient, in humility correcting those who are in opposition, if God perhaps will grant them repentance, so that they may know the truth, and that they may come to their senses and escape the snare of the devil, having been taken captive by him to do his will."* From then on I would endeavour to not argue with a fellow student who was not listening to my arguments anyway. I would rather challenge them on the truths about the Lord Jesus Christ.

This approach was endorsed one Sunday morning. A student had responded to the altar call and the pastor had asked me to pray with him. Before we prayed I asked him if he had any questions. He told me straight away that his head was full of questions about science and the Bible. I promised him that I would visit him in the week to try and answer his questions. Right now I wanted him to ask God's pardon for his pride and sin, accept Jesus Christ as his Saviour, and commit his life to Jesus Christ as his Lord. He understood that and wanted to pray. So we prayed, and the wonderful transaction between Saviour and sinner happened.

When climbing into my car after the service, I asked him for his first question. He thought, and he thought, and he thought. Finally he announced that for some unknown reason he could not think of a single question. That is when I understood in a refreshing way that wonderful Scripture in Hebrews 11:3; *"By faith we understand that the worlds were framed by the word of God, so that the things which are seen were not made of things which are visible."*

Faith in the Lord Jesus Christ produces faith in His infallible Word. I could present scientific argument to my congregations over the years, but I have found that arguments about entropy, thermodynamics, dating techniques and assumptions, and even genetics, passes right over the heads of those who have not studied science. When asked to defend the Bible in the face of intense media opposition, Charles Spurgeon said, "Me, defend the Bible? It is like a lion – let It loose and It will defend Itself!"

Preaching against something, or worse – against someone, taught me some hard lessons. Invariably I felt God's displeasure, and invariably it proved counter-productive. We must be known for what we are *for* rather than what we are *against*.

Preaching against things or persons only feeds the rebel side of human nature. It does not edify, or change, or mature a person. I have found that fabricating or embellishing stories also earns me God's displeasure. I have concluded time after time that I must adequately represent Jesus Christ in His pulpit, and that only the truth – the whole truth – will carry His blessing and change lives.

I also believe that the same Holy Spirit who inspired holy men of old to write every Word of Scripture, must be reverently called upon to anoint the preacher as he preaches and the congregation as they listen. He still works with the Word to confirm it, and He alone gives it its inherent power to change lives. I read that Billy Graham notes that the more he says in his sermons, "The Bible says", the more sinners come to their Saviour when the altar call is given. I believe too that each sermon must be soaked in prayer, and well prepared. I have struggled many times to secure a theme from God for a sermon. Sometimes I get it weeks in advance. Rarely it has come during the worship prior to when I must preach. I far prefer the former. After all, the Holy Spirit knows the end from the beginning. He knows well in advance what He wants for Christ's own. I have also learned, as one seasoned preacher put it, "A particular sermon may take two hours to research and write out, but it takes years of walking with the Lord to truly prepare."

I believe what Pastor Bob taught us at Bible College. He said, "If a sermon is good enough to preach once, it is good enough to preach again!" Invariably the repeats come across differently. So many of my sermons I have gleaned from good sermons I have heard, and good books I have read. I believe that reading is part of my work-load as a pastor.

✝CHAPTER 7

Lessons from Funerals

only conducted one funeral whilst in my first pastorate. It was my first and it was a steep learning curve. We had had a short teaching at Bible College on how best to conduct a funeral, and I had only ever attended one funeral before – and that was my own father's in December, 1978. I received a phone call from Penny in Gweru. She told me that a parent of a toddler in her crèche was seeking a minister to visit his dying father in Kwe Kwe. She told me the name, phone number, and address. I immediately phoned and was around at the house within about twenty minutes. I was met at the door by the dying man's wife. When I announced who I was she gave me a full-on hug as she thanked me profusely for coming. She then clung to me for the entire visit. She took me to her husband's bedside.

He was either in a coma or a deep sleep as he gave me no response when I spoke to him. His wife began to weep, and held me even tighter. I then offered to pray for him. I called on my Saviour to save his blood-bought soul, and then said, "Mr Symons, if you can hear me then please repeat this prayer after me", and I led him in the sinner's prayer. I told him that if he had asked the Lord Jesus from his heart to forgive him all his past sins, then according to the Bible, the Lord Jesus had done just that. If he had received Jesus into his heart as his Saviour, then God, according to the Bible, had made him His child and given him eternal life. If he died now he would go to heaven. I then prayed for God's comfort and strength to be with his wife and family.

I do not know whether there was a transaction between Saviour and sinner – if there was, we'll meet again in heaven one day. He died that night. His widow asked me to conduct the funeral, so the next day the family gathered. I visited them to find out all about the deceased so that I could deliver a personal eulogy. The son from Gweru was beside himself with grief. As he walked me back to my car I put my hand on his shoulder and invited him to talk to me about it.

"You will never understand!" he exclaimed.

"Try me," I replied, "My dad died three and a half years ago."

He swung around to face me as he blurted out, "My father did a business deal over my head, so I phoned him, and hurled all kinds of abuse at him. I tore him to pieces! When I was finished he asked me if that was all, and said goodbye. That was the last time I spoke to him!" He then broke down weeping and I put my arm around his shoulder. I did not know what to say. We parted without saying another word.

The family wanted a cremation at the Warren Hills Crematorium in Harare, a two hour journey away. So I travelled up the day before so that I could familiarise myself with the crematorium before the service. It was very hard for me as that was where my dad's final service was held. The attendant showed me how to press the button on the pulpit to lower the coffin. He also asked me for the hymns to be sung, and he warned me that there is a cremation on the hour, every hour – so I must finish the whole service in half an hour.

I was early for the service the next day. I was there to greet the family car and usher the widow and her family to the front. On the way up the aisle the son asked me to not lower the coffin. It would be too much for him to bear, and his mom had agreed. I was both nervous and emotional as I prayed, sang, gave the eulogy and short message, and as I read the committal. I led the family out to the entrance, and stood by as the other mourners filed past, hugging the family members. One of those that filed past came across to me and sternly told me that I had forgotten to lower the coffin.

"I was requested not to by the family," I replied calmly. He did not know what to say then, and he slunk away.

As I was about to leave, the funeral director placed an envelope in my sweaty hand, and thanked me for the service. I had kept good time! When in the car I opened the envelope to find just five dollars in it. It did not even cover my petrol costs one way from Redcliff, let alone reward me for anything else. I had to remind myself that I was serving God in what I had done. That was a lesson I would often remind myself of, especially when I felt unappreciated or undervalued. I never heard from that family again, even though I had offered to visit them if they requested.

My next funeral was shortly after we had settled in Harare. One day we had a visit from Mark and Sheila. They had been faithful members of our Kwe Kwe Church. He had been a head teacher of a primary school in a small mining village near Kwe Kwe and he was now taking up the post of head teacher of a Christian School in the USA. They were about to catch a flight to the USA, and were desperate to sell their VW Camper. Would we buy it? When we said we could not afford it, they asked us to simply take over the monthly payments – and if we did not want that, then would we please sell it and square up with the previous owners, Ian and Tracy. We agreed and I phoned Ian and Tracy for a meeting to discuss it all. Ian was in a wheel-chair and they had sold the camper because of his deteriorating health. At that meeting they asked me whether they could attend our church, and the next Sunday they came.

I normally visited anyone who had attended our church for two Sundays, but I felt an urge to visit them after their first attendance. So that Wednesday I visited them in their static caravan and, by the pure grace of God, both heeded the glorious Gospel message, and surrendered to the claims of Christ to their lives. That Friday Ian died! It left me in awe of God's intervention and timing! Tracy became a very loyal member of our church for all the time we were in Harare.

Twenty-eight years later Mark visited family in the UK. We happened to be visiting our son down south at the time so we met up. In the course of catching up, I asked him whether he remembered leaving the VW camper with us. He did. I then told him that he could not sell it because God wanted me to meet up with Ian and Tracy. He wanted them to be in church that Sunday, and He wanted me to break with my normal protocol and visit them on the Wednesday, because He wanted to save them by His grace before Ian died on the Friday! Martin too was awed by God's grace!

I was to conduct a great many funerals in Harare. The Lord graciously provided me with opportunities to lead many to Christ on their deathbeds. The family would then ask me to conduct the funeral. I soon came to count it a huge privilege to conduct a Christian's funeral. I turned it into a triumphant affair and a thanksgiving service. The funerals where I was not certain that the deceased was born-again have always been more difficult to conduct. I have never wanted to give any one of the mourners false hope. So my focus has been more on showing the mourners real love and sympathy.

The Bible describes death as *"the last enemy"*, and that is why we fight it so hard. It comes as a thief, and the loss it inflicts can be unbearable for those who have no hope of meeting the loved one again. The emotion I have displayed, and tears I have shed at funerals have been real. They have certainly endeared me to many a mourner. The Bible says that we must rejoice with those who rejoice, and *"weep with those who weep"*.

When the Lord Jesus saw the weeping crowd that had followed

Mary to her brother Lazarus' grave, we have the shortest verse of God's Word – *"Jesus wept"*. One of the big reasons why I shed tears at a funeral of someone I am not sure has gone to heaven, is on account of Christ's sacrifice for him/her having been in vain. I have also taken the opportunity at funerals to sensitively share the death and resurrection of the Lord Jesus to secure eternal life for all who will surrender to His claim to their lives. I know that this has not been well received by some attending a funeral. If looks could kill, I would have died many times over as I stood opposite the "principal mourners" at the exit of the chapel or church. I have always seen the family before to acquire a eulogy from them that mixes facts, gratitude and some humour surrounding their memories of their loved one. If the deceased was a Christian I mix into the eulogy their testimony of God's saving and blessing grace. If they are not Christian, I leave the short Gospel message to a short epilogue before the committal. If there is a reception or wake after the funeral I have always attended. I also have always offered to follow up the "principal mourners". Sadly that offer has often not been taken up. My hands are *open*.

One of the saddest funerals that I conducted was of a two year old little boy. I had visited his parents about two weeks before he died. They were living in squalor. They did not have any beds, nor much other furniture. They did have blankets, and they must all have slept on the cold concrete floor. The father told me that he now had employment in Botswana and asked me for $100 to tide them over until he received his first pay-cheque. I noticed their two-year old was coughing, and I offered to take him for treatment. They assured me that they were taking good care of him. I prayed for them and especially for the little fellow before I left them with the money they had requested. Within days I received the phone-call that the little boy had died. Would I conduct his funeral? I visited them to minister to them in their loss, and to put a eulogy together that would bring them some comfort. The autopsy confirmed he had died of double pneumonia. I suffered deep regret that I had not gone with my premonition and insisted on a visit to the hospital, instead of only forking out those $100. I learned then the lesson that one must never take risks with a child's health!

The extended family rallied around these grieving parents to pay for their son's funeral, and to see to better living conditions for their remaining four-year old. I struggled to conduct that service. I struggled to hold my emotions together. Then when I announced the committal – before I had pressed the button to lower the tiny coffin, the little boy's mother let out a blood-chilling wail. The atmosphere there in the Warren Hills Crematorium became electrified. I paused until those nearest her had calmed her down. I wondered whether I should press the button at all. Instinctively though I knew it would help bring closure even if it was unbearable. So I asked everyone to bow their heads in prayer and I then pressed the button. To my horror the mechanism creaked loudly enough to be heard above my prayer and the mother let out another wail. I paused again until she had calmed down, and then I completed the committal and pronounced the benediction. I knew that that poor woman's grief was multiplied by her profound regrets. I also wondered whether her marriage would survive the trauma. The family moved to Botswana and I never heard from them again.

I had the privilege of witnessing so many converts in my hospital ministry – converts that never attended our church as they died shortly after their conversion. If I knew of someone dying I would rush to their bedside and immediately introduce the Saviour to them. Whether or not they turned their lives over to Christ, I always prayed for them out loud at their side. Often that spoke to them as much as any conversation I had had with them. For those I did not pray "the sinners prayer" with, I await heaven to find out whether they did call on the Lord before their final breath.

One of these was my father's mother. I would often visit her at the nursing home. As I came through the door into her private room she would recognise me and say curtly, "Oh it's you again – you can go now!" I would ignore her request and sit beside her, telling her that I had come all this way to see her, and that I had a message to give her before I left. Again and again I would share the Gospel. Again and again she would rudely dismiss it. Then, shortly before she died I got down on my knees and begged her to seek God's forgiveness through trusting in Jesus Christ as her Saviour. She let me say my piece but remained intransigent. She refused my offer of prayer and I left. The nurse told me that she was praying *The Lord's Prayer* shortly before she died. I hope God had mercy on her, and that I'll meet her in heaven! Nevertheless it was a hard funeral to conduct!

The saddest funeral I have conducted was the funeral of Dennis, a bachelor in his late thirties. His father had been a marine who could not cope with civilian life so he took the drink culture of the armed forces to a new level and became addicted to alcohol. He ended up in a sanitarium. As a teenager Dennis used to visit him there. His father died of cirrhosis of the liver. Dennis had regarded him as his hero, and he took his death very hard. We are not sure when or why he became a "manic depressive". They call it bi-polar nowadays. When he was "up" he was really up – he was full of excitement and you could not stop him talking – or singing. When he was down he was suicidal, and you could not get him talking or singing. Dennis was seldom balanced.

He was in the Hailsford church when we arrived. His trade was in carpentry and decoration. He befriended us from the outset and we grew to really love him. As he was accident-prone he would amuse us with amazing stories of his mishaps. One day Clare told him that she would write a book about him. From then on, whenever something funny or strange happened to him he would excitedly tell Clare, "I have another story for your book about me!"

Dennis was very slow in his work. He was a perfectionist, and his catch-phrase was "you cannot rush a masterpiece!" When he was "up" he would talk to his clients rather than get on with the job on hand. When he was down he would daydream and hardly lift a finger throughout the day. Hence he took longer than any of his colleagues doing the same work. If he had priced up the work (and he was not good at any form of administration), he would take so long over the work as to negate any profit. Some of his clients would get impatient with him saying such things as "I am not paying you to talk to me!" or even, "I did not employ you to preach to me!" If he upset a client he would rapidly descend into a low mood.

I remember once he was challenged by the son of an elderly client over the price he had charged her to replace a door. He had charged her over £900 and taken two full days. It was at the time when the BBC were exposing "rogue traders" that had "ripped off" unsuspecting clients. Dennis became suicidal. Fortunately I heard about it from our organist who was trying in vain to lift his spirits. I spent hours talking him out of what he had been planning. Eventually he took my advice to apologise to the family, and reimburse the lady the difference between his cost and the cost she would have had from another carpenter. He was also desperate to find a suitable wife and have a family of his own. He saw his close friends find wonderful wives and this only served to exaggerate his aloneness.

I was not the only one to spend hours trying to cheer Dennis up when he became depressed. He had wonderful friends in Stuart, Calum, Phil, and Ivan too. Our organist was also a shoulder for him to cry on. She would often have him around for meals, would often help him with mundane things, and would employ him for various maintenance work in her home. An ex-missionary lady in our church would help him with his invoicing, administration, and income-tax returns. The church were his family and the sincere love was mutual.

It was in the last month of our first sabbatical, when we had run out of money and so were "lying low" at home, that Ivan phoned me. "I am so sorry to phone you when you are on sabbatical, John," he began, "but I have news that I must tell you in person. Can I come and see you right away?"

His tone told me that it must be seriously bad news. However I was not prepared for it when he blurted it out on his arrival at our home. "It's Dennis, John," he began emotionally, his voice quivering. "He committed suicide this afternoon." Clare and I stood there in stunned silence. "His sister Jill phoned me shortly after the police had been and gone," Ivan continued slowly and deliberately. Clare and I both began crying. "I cannot handle this one John, but I will help you, if you want me to," he concluded. Clare and I embraced Ivan as he too lost his composure and cried with us.

Over a cup of tea Ivan told us all that he knew. He said that Calum and Stuart were alerted to Dennis' state of mind when they received a call from the hospital. He had been found in his car on a lonely road near Hailsford. He had attempted to overdose on pills. He had not been successful, and had had a stomach-pump and a short stay in hospital. He had written a suicide note saying that everyone would be better-off without him. Jill, who was his next-of-kin, had been informed and she was on her way to collect him. She had been charged to not let him out of her sight. When Jill phoned Ivan she was too emotional to give him details.

Ivan gave me Jill's phone number and I phoned her for an appointment to see her. She was keen to see me straight away. So we travelled down to her country home that evening.

"I am so very sorry," I said as I embraced Jill on arrival at her home. "I just do not know what to say to you!" She would have seen fresh tears filling my eyes as she looked up at me.

"I am grateful that you have come," she replied. "Can I get you a cup of tea?"

It was only when we sat at her breakfast table in her big kitchen that we began to speak again. Once she got going there was no stopping her. "I fetched Dennis from the hospital yesterday afternoon," she began. "He was very quiet, but also apologetic for the trouble he had been. I assured him that I loved him and was grateful that I still had him. He did not want to talk about reasons for his attempt to end his life. I felt I must not press him. So I talked about positive things, hoping to give him a reason to live. My husband is away on business and will return tomorrow. He is an atheist and this will only strengthen his beliefs. This has rocked any vestige of faith in me too."

She stopped for a moment to straighten out her thoughts and refocus on events. Clare, Ivan and I kept quiet as an encouragement for her to spill it all out.

"We had a nice meal last night, Dennis, my two sons Terry and Steve, and I. Dennis was exhausted, he spoke very little, and he took himself off to bed shortly afterwards. I had already told Terry and Steve about Dennis' attempt – and we had agreed to all keep an eye on him. Terry and Steve loved their uncle Dennis." She was digressing again. "They have had a lot of fun through the years ... especially when Dennis has been in an 'up mood'. I hardly slept a wink last night as I listened carefully to make sure he did not leave his room."

She then told us how that at about 12 noon she received a phone-call. She left Dennis in the lounge whilst she took the call in the hallway. When she returned to the lounge he was gone. She panicked and shouted for him. No reply. Terry and Steve came running in when they heard her shout. They then ran out to search the garden and the woods nearby. Steve, the younger of her teenagers, found Dennis hanging by a rope from a horizontal branch. His feet were inches from the ground. He must have sized up the tree and planned the exact length of rope. Steve lifted Dennis' limp body and shouted to Terry to bring a sharp knife. Terry went hysterical when he rushed into the kitchen to tell his mom and grab a knife. She phoned 999 asking for an ambulance and the police. They responded very quickly, but too late.

We assured her that she was not in any way to blame. Dennis had made the decision, not her. From Clare's counselling training she knew that people who are going to commit suicide tend to narrow down all the options to that one – to end their life. It is like they get tunnel vision. They can only see one way out. It means that they rule out everyone and everything else. Once they are determined to take their life, there is very little anyone can do or say to deter them. It is the end of an obsession.

Jill insisted that she had failed him somehow. I said sincerely that I also felt that way. Ivan and Clare said the same. That night when I phoned Calum and Stuart they said the same. Our organist took it worse than all of us. She was inconsolable for months. It seemed the whole church went into meltdown. It was traumatic. Clare and I came off sabbatical for two weeks as we tried to piece things together with a deeply wounded congregation.

Jill naturally asked me to conduct the funeral. Clare and I spent an afternoon with her and her family in order to put together a eulogy, and order of service. He was to be buried at a small village church where his mom and dad were buried. Calum offered to sort out Dennis' flat, and Jill was very grateful for that. He readily accepted my offer to help him. That was a harrowing experience.

The funeral directors lived on a farm, and they kept Dennis' body in a converted garage. Calum wanted to see him there so I offered to accompany him. I did not go in to see Dennis' body. I simply waited outside whilst Calum spent ten to fifteen minutes in the room.

A number of my colleagues from the Minister's Fraternal came to the funeral in support, and the majority of our church took the day off work to pay their respects. Most importantly I felt the Lord's comforting presence. I believe that so many others did too. He is the source of all comfort (2 Corinthians 1:3,4). The Holy Spirit certainly helped me in the part I played that day. To this day I believe that a suicide funeral is the hardest funeral to conduct. As Selwyn Hughes, the Christian counsellor and writer of the *Every Day with*

Jesus series says, "The thing that aggravates grief most are the regrets, the 'If only's.'" Suicides tend to give those regrets in bucket-loads. Incidentally, it was the suicide of a young man Selwyn Hughes had tried to counsel that stirred him up to study counselling in depth, and so come up with his excellent counselling model used by *Crusade for World Revival* (CWR) to this day.

When Pastor Bob heard about the suicide he phoned me from South Africa to give me his condolences. He knew Dennis from a couple of his visits to Hailsford. Each time he had preached at our church Dennis had gone forward for prayer. What Pastor Bob said to me on that phone-call brought huge comfort to me. He told me that in the forty years of his ministry he had never had the trial of a suicide in his church. Then he said, "It must have been very hard for you, John!" That sentence, in an inexplicable way, brought me a great deal of comfort.

✝CHAPTER 8

Lessons in the Exercise of Authority as a Minister of the Gospel

A dramatic thing happened whilst at Redcliff. I had a visit from Lisa whom I had led in the sinner's prayer whilst I was at Bible College. She brought to our house her sister's brother-in-law, Bruce, and asked me to explain to him how he could become a Christian. I explained the Gospel and he ended the afternoon praying the sinner's prayer too. However, as they walked to the car I spotted them briefly holding hands. That really upset me as I had also led her husband Shaun to say the sinner's prayer when I was at Bible College.

The next day Shaun arrived at my home in his land-cruiser. He remained in the driver's seat so I went out to meet him. He was trembling with rage. On his lap was a 9mm pistol.

"Hello Shaun...What's going on?" I asked as I opened the door for him.

"My wife has told me she has fallen in love with her sister's brother-in-law, and I was on my way to kill him. As I got to the Redcliff turn-off I felt a strong urge to see you first. You will need to give me a b****y good reason to not kill the b****d."

By the time we had finished a cup of tea together Shaun had calmed down. I promised him that I would see Bruce that night, and have a straight man-to-man talk with him. I would let Shaun know the outcome. As a gesture he removed the magazine from his pistol and ejected the round from the breach.

I visited Bruce and Lisa that night, and asked to speak to Bruce alone. I told him that although I was young enough to be his son, I was coming to him as a minister of the Gospel of the Lord Jesus Christ. He told me that he respected that. However whilst I spoke calmly and assertively, he spoke loudly so as to be overheard by Lisa in the kitchen. Sometimes he would re-iterate what I had said so that Lisa could hear.

As I was getting nowhere, I offered to pray for the situation. He asked me not to pray a biased prayer! He obviously did respect my high office as a minister of the Gospel! In the prayer I asked the Lord to bring His conviction to bear on both Lisa and Bruce. I reminded the Lord that both were answerable to Him, and that one day they would both stand before His judgement seat to give an account. When I opened my eyes I could not help notice that Bruce was trembling.

"You are right, Pastor, I will ask Lisa to go back to Shaun and rebuild their marriage. That would be the right and loving thing to do."

That night he told her. She told him that he could dismiss her but that she would never return to Shaun. So he embraced her again and phoned me the next day to tell me that he had made up his mind, whether it angered the Lord or not, to commit to Lisa. I then had the task of calming Shaun down until he backed off, and put away his gun.

Lisa and Bruce never came to our church, and Shaun returned to his farm near Bulawayo.

The lessons I learned were to intervene when life is threatened and to stay the course until the threat is averted. If Shaun had not put his gun away I would most certainly have called the police! I also learned that I had respect in my office as a Minister of the Gospel. I need to believe that that respect is to be expected of people like Bruce who was old enough to be my father – and of those much younger than I. My dress has always been at minimum smart-casual, my demeanour has never been sloppy, nor my speech coarse or crude, and my timing has been punctual – in order to command respect too. God describes my calling as a *high and holy* one and I must believe and live it!

One Sunday morning service we had a visit from Ivan, a man in his mid-twenties. He told me that he was searching for the meaning of life. It took a couple of sessions with me before he was convinced that the Lord Jesus had a claim on his life. Christ fully purchased him on Calvary's Cross. I believe that central to the Gospel story is the transaction on that old rugged cross, and I believe a "cross-less" Gospel is a false Gospel. Seeing our God laying our iniquity on His Son in the greatest demonstration of love ever and then repenting sincerely of that iniquity, is altogether necessary for a sound conversion. Well, Ivan placed his life in Christ's nail-scared hands and repented.

He was baptised in water and the Holy Spirit, and became a faithful member of our fellowship. Although I had visited his home to speak with his wife Yvette, she had shown no interest in spiritual things. However, he became a very frequent visitor to our home. Straight after work he'd be around for a chat and prayer. I became weary of this and asked him why he did not go straight home to his now pregnant wife. Before his conversion he would drop by a hotel for a couple of drinks before returning home. She was used to having him back later. I warned him that the number one reason for a wife having an affair was neglect by her husband.

One Saturday I took him to play a round of golf. We were in the car when he told me that they had a lodger that kept his wife company. Although I initially presumed it would be a female lodger, I asked him nevertheless to tell me about her. Oh, "she" was a male medical student. I flared with anger at how naive Ivan was, and I told him to "wake up and smell the coffee!"

The following Tuesday he returned home early to find Yvette in bed with their lodger! On account of his embarrassment at not heeding my warnings, he did not contact me until the next afternoon. "Please get me out of here!" he pleaded over the phone.

Surprised I replied, "Get you out of where?"

"I have been committed to Ward 12, the Psychiatric Ward! It is hell in here!"

"But why are you there?" I asked.

"My work colleagues noticed how depressed I was when I came to work this morning (he worked at the hospital), and they called in the psychiatrist who drugged me up, and committed me to this hell-hole!"

"Why were you so depressed, Ivan?" I had remembered how happy he was on Sunday when I last saw him.

I knew of his severe embarrassment when he whispered, "I found Yvette in bed with our lodger!"

I agreed to talk to his psychiatrist when he told me that she was there in her office at Ward 12. When I arrived at the main door to this ward, I heard a loud voice from inside the room next to the door. That room had a small window set high up on the wall. There was no way that the patient in that room could have seen me arrive. Yet he shouted, "Man of God, get me out of here!" I rang the bell for an attendant to unlock the door and allow me access. Whilst waiting the patient shouted again, saying the same words. It sent a shiver down my spine. How did he know that I was a man of God? The attendant asked my business and took me down the passage past that room. Its door was made of steel and had a small sliding cover over a small window. The patient cried out once more, "Man of God, get me out of here!" as I passed. This surprised the attendant who turned to give me the "up and down look". I learned later that that room was a padded cell.

The psychiatrist did not seem pleased to see me, and wanted me out as soon as possible. I told her that Ivan needed a good friend, not drugs and a stay in Ward 12. She asked me what I knew about psychiatry. I was struck by the power over human souls she seemed to have. Standing by her were two burly attendants, and I gained the impression that at a word she could order them to carry me out of the building. She refused to release Ivan. That is when I became angry. I had never done this before or since, but I told her that I may not be a qualified psychiatrist but that *I was a minister of the Gospel of Jesus Christ*. I also told her that I was an intelligent man who possessed a Bachelor of Science Degree. I was not a man who was in the ministry because I was not able to secure any other employment.

I believe she felt I would not be intimidated by her – and that I would not leave Ward 12 without Ivan. She then told me that she would release Ivan on condition that he is in my charge 24 hours a day for the next week, that he reported to her every day, and that I ensured he took his medication. Then she warned me that if these conditions were not met she would have the police visiting me to restore him to Ward 12.

In the car Ivan was very repentant for having been so naive, and for having ignored my warnings. He was truly shocked when I asked him what he had done to his lodger. "Nothing! I just walked out of the room...what did you expect me to do to him?" he asked.

"I expected you to beat him up and throw him out!" I somewhat angrily replied. Ivan was horrified.

"And you call yourself a Christian...and a minister of the Gospel? I cannot believe what I have just heard...you expected me to beat him up?"

"I believe that if you had done that, Yvette would have realised that you love her. Just walking away proved the opposite," I replied.

"Is that what you would do if you found a man taking advantage of Clare?" he asked.

"If a man took advantage of Clare in any way it would be 'gloves off', it would be 'open season'. No man can touch her like that. And she knows that!"

"And I thought that it was a Christian thing to simply walk out of that room!" he said softly. I told him that God is a jealous God and that one of His names is "Jealous" (Exodus 34:14). Then I explained to him that the Hebrew word for jealousy meant "a zeal to protect what to you is very precious". I believed that that kind of jealousy gives backbone to love. I explained that if the insult or injury was against me, I would turn the other cheek and walk away. This injury he witnessed was against his marriage, and if that were precious to him he would do all in his power to protect it.

He and I had taken up arms during the Rhodesian conflict because we had witnessed what Mugabe and Nkomo's terrorists had inflicted on their own people, and we counted Christian civilisation (and innocent human life) precious enough to protect at all costs. I reminded him that the Cross of Calvary was the stage of the greatest battle of all time. The Lord Jesus fought the sin that enslaves us, the devil who tempts and deceives us, and death that will ultimately claim us. His resurrection proves He was victorious over all three! He did that because He counted a relationship with us to be precious enough to create and protect at all costs!

I left him with his thoughts for the rest of the journey home. He stayed in our home for a week. He recovered, was taken off his medication which made him feel like a zombie, and he was discharged by his psychiatrist. Interestingly, I went to see Yvette at her work. She was a manager at an airline company. I was shown to her private office. I knocked at her door, she told me to come in, and as soon as she saw me she burst into tears. She told me that she felt so ashamed of herself for her adultery.

Her lodger spent hours talking to her and one thing led to another, until things went too far. I asked her what she would have felt if Ivan had dragged her lodger out of the bed and beat him up. "I would have felt that Ivan loved me!" she replied. It was hard for me to witness her pain. I offered to pray for her before I left, and she accepted my offer.

She saw no hope for her marriage and so they separated. Their baby was born before the divorce came through. I never did see her again, and after a while I stopped asking Ivan about her and their daughter.

The lessons I learned were that I was right to warn Ivan to spend more time with his wife, even if that meant less time with me or even with the church. I learned that I should have used my authority as Christ's minister to insist that he spent more time with her. I also learned that demons recognise my authority in Christ – they must have made that poor soul in that padded cell cry out, "Man of God, get me out of here!" How else would he have known who I was? Finally I learned that I can and must not be intimidated by others, even if they are professionals, and powerful like that psychiatrist. If I walk in the fear of the Lord and comfort of the Holy Spirit as the early church did (Acts 9:31) I would have no one, and nothing, to fear. So long as I also remain humble like my Saviour!

My father was a "civil servant". His title was District Commissioner. In that role he both served those in his charge *and* carried an authority that was well respected. Even so I recognised that I was a servant who *thereby* carried authority! I learned not to be "a push-over". Perhaps I was a bit strong about beating up a rival – but I was right for the sentiment as proved by Yvette's response to my question!

†CHAPTER 9

Lessons on Sexual Temptation

I can tell of one incident that happened on a pastoral visit in Kwe Kwe. I had arranged to visit a young married couple one afternoon. When I arrived, I discovered only the wife was there.

"Where is your husband?" I asked.

"He has been called away. Please come in anyway."

"No!" I replied, "I'll make an appointment to see you again when he is in."

"Please at least see the photos of the safari we've just returned from," she pleaded. Innocently, I agreed, and there by my car she showed me a number of photographs, but she stopped and giggled as she showed me a compromising photograph of herself climbing out of the back of a truck. That verse in *The Lord's Prayer* that says *"lead us not into temptation, but deliver us from the evil one"*, came to mind and I hastily opened my car door, said a quick goodbye, and sped away.

Another time was in Harare. I was thoroughly discouraged, and that left me very vulnerable to satanic attack. When I was told by Pastor Paul that I had no alternative but leave the ministry (this story is told later in this book), I had a surprise visit from Brenda. She and her husband were members of our house-group, and Clare and I were very fond of them both. She rang the bell at the gate and I went out to meet her. She took one look at my tear-stained face and bloodshot eyes and, although we remained at my gate, speaking through the bars, I felt that what we shared then created a dangerous emotional bond.

When Clare returned from work that lunchtime I told her everything. She flung her arms around me. The love and support I felt from my dear wife broke for me the tie to Brenda completely. However Brenda still needed to extract herself. Not long after the gate conversation she asked us to fetch her for house-group. Her husband was away on business and had taken their family car. When we dropped her back at her home afterwards Clare said to me, "If I did not know better, I would think that there is something going on between you and Brenda." She was commenting on the way Brenda was looking at me when we said goodbye. So the next day I visited Brenda in her home. I showed her no physical affection and very quickly told her what Clare had noticed. I then told her that I simply adored Clare, and would pursue no relationship that would destroy her love and respect for me. I admitted that I had felt an emotional bond form at the gate, but for me that had been broken when I saw Clare again. Brenda told me how relieved she was that I had had the courage to tell her all this. She admitted the bond and was glad it would go no further. She then reaffirmed her love for her really good husband. We parted as good and grateful friends.

I recalled clearly the parable I had been taught by Pastor Bob at Bible College. He told us that at the end of time Satan has a sale of all the weapons that he had used against the children of God down through the ages. On the tables were weapons like lying, cheating, thieving, gossip, slander, adultery, fornication, licentiousness, anger, bitterness, resentment, cynicism, unbelief, fear, anxiety, panic, despair, isolation, hatred and so on. Set apart on its own was a glass case enclosing a wedge-shaped instrument that looked very well used. It was fetching a far higher price than all the other weapons put together. When asked why, Satan said that it had been his favourite weapon. If he could get in the door with that weapon, he would be free to use any of the other weapons laid out on the tables. The weapon was called "discouragement"!

I also remembered Pastor Bob's last words to me as he said goodbye when I left Bible College. He told me to guard against discouragement. The big lesson I have learned over and over again is that should I not receive encouragement from others, including my wife, I must to be sure to *encourage myself in the Lord*" (1 Samuel 30:6 in KJV).

Sexual temptation is "Every Man's Battle" and I have been no exception. One of my best friends told me that his addiction to internet pornography had been discovered by his daughters and their husbands. They had seen it in the history of his web browsing. He had to sincerely repent before his lovely wife and his immediate family. I was shocked as I never expected him to even dabble in that seedy world. I told him that by God's grace I had never looked at internet porn (although I had often been tempted "out of curiosity"). He told me how blessed I was. I then realised the danger of even looking once. If he could become addicted, it scared me that I could too. I am grateful that I did not learn that lesson the hard way like my friend. The outcome of his repentance was the sound conversion of two of his daughters and their husbands.

The lessons I have learned are to work hard at my marriage; make it obvious to everyone else that I really love my wife; and "nip in the bud" any inappropriate attraction. Christian ladies have an added beauty from their relationship with our Saviour and Lord (2 Corinthians 2:15). We can call them beautiful because God does! (See Genesis 6:2; 12:14; 24:16; 29:17; 2 Samuel 11:2; 14:27 and so on). Too many beautiful Christian ladies have left a local church because they have interpreted signals from a church leader that he is "grooming her for an affair".

About a month after starting in Harare, Clare decided to tidy up the cupboards at the one end of the vestry/Sunday School room. We found minutes of elder's meetings, files of church records and accounts, Sunday School materials and books. Among the books was the classic by Andrew Murray entitled *Humility*. I was intrigued by the title as I had never before seen a book devoted to that subject. So as soon as I could I read, and re-read it. I was especially intrigued by his chapter on the humility of the Lord Jesus. I saw that pride is the mother of all sin and evil, and that it was from pride that Jesus came primarily to redeem us. Humility became the quality I most admired the Lord Jesus for, and humility became my great aspiration in my quest to represent the Lord Jesus adequately. Working that out in practice has been my greatest challenge over the years.

Shortly after reading *Humility* I attended a life-changing minister's fraternal. A missionary had come out from America to hold special meetings in Zimbabwe. On account of him being there a number of Zimbabwe-based missionaries were also in attendance. He began by telling us what he believed God was doing in America. He started by declaring that the most important thing to God is character. He said that God, in His mercy towards the large crowds drawn to their meetings, had been using men and women of questionable character. They made up stories, exaggerated their success and told outright lies; they were self-centred, arrogant, self-serving and boastful; they were greedy and extravagant. Much of their sermons were devoted to coercing their audience to part with their hard-earned cash. He said that they had "professionalized" the ministry – and would not take up a calling unless they were paid well, were given a generous travel and holiday allowance and so on.

He then went on to say that in the small churches of America there are men and women that have been touched by Calvary love. They are currently going through the fires of trials and hardship. They are Christ-centred, humble people who are not in the ministry for fame and finance. They will not even exaggerate let alone tell bold-faced lies. They are Christ-like, and God has been preparing them for end-time harvest ministry. "You watch," he continued, *"God will soon expose those misrepresenting His character. Then He will bring out of the wings and on to centre stage those that He can trust – those He has been preparing in the fires. So take courage any here who are going through the refining fire. Hang in there! Seek Him and trust Him! Your time is coming! "He who continually goes forth weeping, bearing seed for sowing, shall **doubtless** come again with rejoicing, bringing his sheaves with him,"* (Psalm 126:6).

His prophecy began to come true shortly afterwards with the exposure and expulsion of many well-known American ministers. It happened soon enough in Harare too. I still wonder why God showed me, a 28 year old pastor of a small struggling church, the vivid dream I had one night. I saw Pastor Harry, a local pastor, in the pulpit of his church. He was telling his six hundred or so members that he had heard of criticism of himself and others in the church. He told any critic to please leave the church, and assured them that there were plenty of people who could and would take their place. Then I saw his wife (I had not ever met her but I instinctively knew she was his wife) leaving the platform with the guitarist, a man much younger than her, and they went out the side door into a dark night. Pastor Harry then came off the platform to take the arm of a married women who had been sitting by her husband in the front row. They also left the church by a side door and disappeared into the darkness of night. The dream concluded with a dispersal of the church and I saw in my dream two couples coming for refuge to our church. I woke up in a sweat. I remembered every detail of the dream and instinctively knew God had given it to me.

I was so deeply troubled by the dream that I found out where Pastor Harry lived and I went to his home to tell him. However I was too nervous. I parked up a little distance from his driveway. I respected Pastor Harry. He had been good to me. He had validated my ministry in front of the other ministers in the fraternal. We also hardly knew each other, and I was the new-boy in the ministry. I asked God a number of times, "Why me?" I asked Him for courage when His silence told me He had His reasons. I reasoned that as I was an intercessor, the dream was for me to intercede before God's throne of grace for Pastor Harry, his wife, and his church. I am ashamed to say that after some time of dithering I started up my car, and drove back home.

I asked the Lord to arrange a meeting with Pastor Harry if He wanted me to tell him the dream. That night I had another vivid dream. I saw the city in darkness and evenly spread around were buildings with light. I was taken into one of those buildings. It was a small church with a congregation listening intently to their pastor preaching. I felt the light represented involvement. I came out of the church to once again look over the city. It was then I noticed a large building that was dimly lit. I was taken there. It was a large church with a big wide platform. I felt there was a professional praise band there, and the pastor striding up and down the platform looked very self-assured and assertive. The platform was well lit whereas the congregation was bathed is soft lighting. The dim light I understood represented lack of involvement. I also saw people coming in through the wide doors. I came out of that church to follow where the people were coming from. They were coming from the small churches. I was taken back into a small church where I saw people slipping out of their chairs and leaving. I saw the pastor stop preaching, and hanging his head in disappointment and defeat. I came out of that church to see a giant dark fist forming over the city. I noticed one small church after another disappear. Suddenly the dark fist swooped down on the platform of the big church. Everyone there was sent flying and all lights in the building went out.

This dream only served to re-enforce my previous dream and I feared for the future of the church in Harare.

Day after day the burden for "the" Church increased. I sighed and groaned a lot through the day. At our next fraternal Pastor Harry announced that he was joining his church with another in the city and they would be meeting in the large Avondale Cinema on Sundays. He felt that that was what was best for the church. Listening to him, I felt he was trying to prepare his church for his departure, and this was his way of minimising the fallout. I hung around after the meeting hoping for an opportunity to talk to him, but after engaging with a couple of his colleagues he made a hasty retreat and was gone.

The following week we were all invited to hear a Messianic Jew speak about Christian community. To my amazement Pastor Harry sat in the spare seat beside me, and at the interval he remained seated to speak to me. My heart was racing. This was the opportunity that I had asked God for. I feared missing it so I blurted out, "Pastor Harry, the Lord has laid you very heavily on my heart. It is a big burden I carry for you and I would like you to tell me about it."

"Oh that must be to do with the visits we have been having from the CIO (the Central Intelligence Organisation – Zimbabwe's equivalent to the KGB). Our church building belongs to a man whose son had an armaments factory under the Smith government. Ian Smith (the Rhodesian Prime Minister) had allowed him to dismantle and ship out his enterprise just before Zimbabwe became independent. So the CIO are threatening us with the seizure of our church building."

"No," I tremblingly said, "my burden has nothing to do with the CIO investigations. It has everything to do with you and your wife!"

Pastor Harry abruptly rose from his chair, took up his Bible in his arms, said, "My wife is also worried about the CIO," and he left. I do not know whether he left the building or whether he sat somewhere else after the interval.

I never saw him again.

Two weeks later we were called to a special ministers' fraternal. The new chairman, who was the minister of the church that had combined with Pastor Harry's, announced that Pastor Harry's wife had gone off with a guitarist in her worship band, and Pastor Harry was on his way to Durban, South Africa, with the wife of one of his members. He announced that at least two hundred and fifty of Pastor Harry's church had not turned up for Sunday worship at the cinema. Pastor Harry's church had scattered. Perhaps some may find their way to another church.

It was a very somber meeting, and although God had forewarned me, I was truly heartbroken. I have wondered to this day whether I could have done anything (with God's wisdom and grace) to have averted the catastrophe.

The following Sunday two couples from Pastor Harry's church, the Bodens and the MacLeans, were in our church. The MacLeans told me that for some time they knew something was wrong. For a start, Pastor Harry's wife would lead the worship for an hour to an hour-and-a-half. This, they realised now, was to squeeze out the message that Pastor Harry had prepared. So in hindsight they could tell that there were tensions. Then Pastor Harry's references to criticism and gossip now made sense too. After a couple of months with us the Bodens left to live in South Africa. I had the huge pleasure and privilege of baptising the MacLeans. Despite being members of Pastor Harry's church for many, many years, I guess that the sheer numbers of people there had mitigated against them making that confession of faith earlier.

In Hailsford I had a colleague who also broke his covenant with his wife. Shortly after we had left Hailsford to take up an appointment in Livingston, Scotland, he began an affair which lasted about six months before it was exposed. He left the ministry in disgrace, and his church dispersed. It was another sobering reminder of the very high cost of moral failure. In the secular world the participants seem to get away with it lightly. For a minister of the Gospel there seems to be little mercy. The consequences for all concerned are catastrophic.

† CHAPTER 10

Lessons from an Attempt to Usurp

Richard phoned me from Bulawayo one day to announce that he was leaving the pastorate there, and he, Shirley, and their two children were planning on coming up to Harare to begin another ministry. He explained that he had inherited some land near Harare, and that his "vision" was to create a *School of Ministry*. There he could take in ministers for further training. He knew that we were in our own home now and that the church manse was temporarily occupied by bachelors. Could he and his family live there for a few months whilst the *School of Ministry* project was set up?

He flattered me by telling me that he believed I was the very best pastor he had ever known and he wanted his family to come under my ministry for a while. I was very uncertain about him coming. I questioned him at length about his future plans. He assured me that he had the full approval of both Pastor Charles and Pastor Paul. I felt his growing irritation with my questioning. He promised me it would be three to six months at the most. I eventually conceded. I gave the bachelors notice, and Clare and I worked flat out to completely redecorate the manse for Richard's family.

I knew I was in deep trouble when Richard first climbed out of his car. He hardly greeted me as he walked briskly to the front door of the manse to see where he was bringing his family. Shirley was much more friendly. When we had caught up with him in the lounge, he told me that the whole place would need to be redecorated to be fit for habitation. I was stunned into silence. Shirley detected my disappointment and immediately began to say what a lovely home it would be for them all.

Richard then turned down my offer to help him unload the removals lorry and place his belongings in his new home. He told me that the workers on the lorry had been paid to do the job, and that he would be directing operations. So I returned home wishing that I had been strong enough to turn him down at that first phone call. I had believed him when he told me that his plans had the full endorsement from Pastors Charles and Paul. I now deeply regretted that I had not verified that with them directly. It would only have taken a phone-call!

More trouble came the following Sunday. I was delighted to see Fred and Joanne come to the church for the first time. They had attended a wedding of her niece that I had conducted a couple of weeks before. I had spoken at length to them about the Lord Jesus when we were seated at the same table at the wedding reception. Before we parted they promised to come some day to our church. They sat at the back of our crowded church.

During the worship time Richard stood to his feet and prayed out loud. I say "prayed", but it was more a string of commands and declarations. When Joanne recognised him she nudged her husband, whispered in his ear, and they both stood up and left the church. I had turned to see Richard when he began, and I caught their movement through the corner of my eye. I was seated in the front row of the church so I knew I could not rush out to find out the matter.

Before I preached I came to the Lord's Table for the time of the Breaking of Bread. I gave a short talk on the wonder of the sacrificial death of our Saviour, and I asked my pastor "colleague" to assist in the distribution of the bread and wine. A look of disgust came over his face as he waved his arms and said an audible "No!" So I asked one of my elders instead, and he willingly assisted.

After the service I tackled Richard over his refusal to assist me. He told me that that was the deacon's job, and that he was a pastor, not a deacon. I asked him, "Who served the bread and the wine at the very first communion service?" He had no answer. He looked disdainfully at me and walked away. I was angered at his arrogance.

Clare and I discussed everything when we had time alone together later (we believed strongly in shielding our sons as much as possible from "church politics"). We both became resolute that we would fight to have Richard removed. And that was before I phoned Fred and Joanne to ask them about their sudden exit from the church during our time of worship.

Joanne told me that on the Friday Richard had brought his son into her office to ask for the application form for a provisional driver's license. She had politely explained that they had run out of those application forms, that they were on back-order, and should arrive any day soon. Richard instantly lost his temper. He ranted and raved until she was in tears. There was no way that she could believe that he was a Christian. Neither was there any way that she could now attend the same church as him. I apologised and promised that he would not be long with us. She understood and promised to return when he no longer attended.

I phoned Pastor Paul as soon as I came off the phone to Joanne. He was unsympathetic, saying that I should never have invited Richard to come in the first place. He denied that he had ever endorsed Richard's plans. The problem was mine, not his, and he did not have the time or energy to discuss it further. I could not believe what I was hearing. I told him that if Richard was not asked to leave by our HQ, then I would have no alternative but to resign. That was my choice, he told me. We said goodbye, and I hung up the phone. I felt my whole world was collapsing around me. I was not in a good state of mind or heart when I put pen to paper to write out my resignation letter. I made several mistakes and several attempts before giving up.

I made up my mind that I would never give Richard the pulpit. After the next Sunday morning service, during which he "prayed" a "prayer" containing a message for me and the church, he told me that the people were not being fed by my sermons. The only reason he believed any came to the church was that they thought I was a "nice guy", and they did not want to hurt my feelings. The congregation needed to know "who they were in Christ" and all the "rights" that were now theirs.

The next Sunday he seemed even more frustrated with me. I was hoping by now that he had the message that I did not trust him with the pulpit. After that service I asked him how his plans were proceeding for the *School of Ministry*. He admitted that all his plans had fallen through, and that he was now going to be my assistant minister "whether I liked it or not". I told him that I did not like it, and that I would not have it. He left me with the promise he would be speaking to our HQ about me. I realised then that his flattery of me in that first phone-call was manipulative. Now his threat to take the matter to the HQ was a bully-tactic. I repented before the Lord on account of the first (I should have sought His will before conceding to Richard's request), and I sincerely asked God to help me trust Him in relation to this threat.

That week I set myself a three day fast to intercede for the situation and our future. All that was thrust upon us seemed to have the devil's fingerprints all over. I was looking to God for Him to rise to the battle, and to graciously give us His victory. I felt too weak (because I felt partly to blame for our predicament), to put up a fight.

The next weekend we were hosting Pastor Andrew from Cape Town. He was the guest speaker for a leaders' seminar to be held in our church. We highly respected him so we felt we had to put on a brave face for him. Pastor Paul and Pastor Charles both came to the seminar. As soon as I could arrange a time with them I stated my intention to resign from the church, and seek another ministry within another denomination.

They accepted my resignation, stating that they would have to now put Richard in my place. My eyes welled up with tears. I left the room, which had been my vestry for seven years, a truly broken man. The thief had come to steal, kill and destroy. Where was the Good Shepherd? I was reminded about what Jesus said about the hireling, *"But a hireling, he who is not the shepherd, one who does not own the sheep, sees the wolf coming and leaves the sheep and flees; and the wolf catches the sheep and scatters them. The hireling flees because he is a hireling and does not care about the sheep."* (John 10:12,13) I did care for the sheep! I was not a shepherd for the money! I had laid down my life for the sheep. I would have kept resisting the "wolf" if I had my superiors' support.

They had given me the opposite – in fact I felt betrayed! My mind was in such turmoil. I was so confused. I stood on the platform looking blankly at the chairs in front of me. Just then Richard brushed past me on his way to see the pastors in the vestry. That jolted me into walking out of the church. They told him of my resignation. He offered to fill my position, stating that his ministry was what was needed in Harare. They asked him to return after the meeting that night with his "vision" for the church after I left.

Pastor Andrew was preparing himself in my office, adjacent to the vestry, for the evening session. Whilst I waited to take him home for his supper, Richard came out of the vestry with a triumphant smile. He told me that he believed I had resigned because I needed a break from ministry. In his considered opinion, I needed a time of being ministered to – and he was the perfect one to do that for me. I told him that he alone was the reason for my resignation, and that therefore he would be the last person I would want as my pastor.

In the car Pastor Andrew asked me what was going on. He had overheard a heated debate between Richard and the other pastors, and his assessment was that Richard was "a very dangerous man!" I told him all, including the acceptance of my resignation. He was horrified. He told me in no uncertain terms that he believed God had called me into His ministry. Both Clare and I had preached for him at his church in Cape Town, and he and the church had been truly blessed. There was no way that he would allow this to happen.

Later as he sat down with Clare and I, he told us firmly that we should never make big decisions (such as resigning from a church we loved and cared for) when we were depressed, discouraged, defeated, or in any low emotional state. He asked us to withdraw our resignation immediately. He reiterated his belief that Richard was "a very dangerous man", and said that we should never allow him to take on the congregation we had built up from so very few. Clare and I were hugely encouraged with all the affirmation we received from Pastor Andrew. He was a true God-send. The Good Shepherd was wonderfully watching over us. The timing of Pastor Andrew's visit was simply perfect. God proved again that He knows the end from the beginning and that nothing ever takes Him by surprise.

Richard did not attend that evening seminar. He had spent the time writing out his "vision" for the church. So I saw Pastor Charles and Pastor Paul first. I told them that on the encouragement of Pastor Andrew, Clare and I had been persuaded to withdraw our resignation. They cautiously expressed their delight, and told me that they were expecting Richard any minute to present his "vision" for the church. They would tell him of our decision, and try to work something else out for him.

I met Richard on his way into the church. He was in a hurry, but I managed to tell him that I had withdrawn my resignation as he rushed by. I do not know what went on in that meeting. All I know is that he told me afterwards he would be leaving our church immediately, and he would leave the manse as soon as he could find alternative accommodation. Pastor Andrew had also said something to Pastor Charles and Pastor Paul on our behalf. He congratulated us in the car on the way home, and he further encouraged us.

We soon returned to our normal selves, grateful for the lessons learned, and for the grace of God given. I never told any in the congregation the reasons for the departure of Richard and his family. My worship leader made the comment to me that he felt that there had been a "personality clash" between Richard and I that he would have liked to mediate. That made me question whether Richard came across as a "get-up-and-go-for-it" pastor, and that my "get-up-and-go" had to some extent "got up and gone".

†CHAPTER 11

When People Leave the Church

Redcliff and Harare had proved to be a very hard assignment. Throughout our time there, Zimbabwe was haemorrhaging its white population. Many of our new converts emigrated. Many Christians who found in us their spiritual home also emigrated. We would involve some enthusiast in a ministry like Sunday School teaching and before long they were dropping out because they were emigrating. The forming of friendships within the church was crucial to some – and if they failed to do that then they were off to a friend's church or to a bigger church where the possibilities of friendships were greater. It was always hard to lose people who meant so much to us. It was not easy to keep *open hands*, when we could see how unsettled the remaining church members became when people left for whatever reason, but especially when they left for another local church.

Janet was a faithful member of our Harare Church from when we first arrived. Her husband Edward was not a Christian, although he was very happy that she was. Clare and I spent much time visiting them, and I became Edward's firm friend. I would often challenge him to surrender to the Lord Jesus Christ. Janet was convinced he was moving in the right direction and that soon he would walk with Jesus besides her.

Then came that terrible Sunday morning. Edward phoned to ask me to fetch Janet for church. She had confessed to a one-night stand with a friend of theirs and he did not trust her with the family car. I was very grateful that he believed that the church and I could help restore Janet to her covenant relationship with him. Clare and our sons went to church in our car as she needed to set up for the worship and the Sunday School. I fetched Janet in the church car. The six mile journey from their home to the church was one of the most awkward journeys of my life. She was truly ashamed of her sin. I spoke of God's forgiveness that was purchased in full on Calvary's Cross. I also told her that we loved them both and would work with them to restore trust and respect. She was in no mood to speak freely and there were long awkward silences. After the service I took our sons home and Clare returned Janet to hers.

However Janet's guilt and shame drove a wedge between us. Our visits to pastorally counsel them were difficult. Her attendance at our church became reluctant and unhappy, even though no-one else there knew of her sin. Then came the day when she told me bluntly that she was leaving our church to attend the Rhema Church. It had "far more to offer" her. To this day I regret asking her whether she was grateful for our ministry to her and her family over the years. She fired back, "You are the ones who should be grateful that I stuck it out here for so long!" I learned a big lesson then. Paul said in 2 Corinthians 12:15, *"And I will very gladly spend and be spent for your souls; though the more abundantly I love you, the less I am loved."* Ever since then I have prayed for the marriages in my churches. I have also not asked for thanks when someone leaves my church and life.

We had been in the ministry for two years when Pastor Charles' son-in-law Paul returned from *Christ For All Nations* Bible Institute in Dallas, Texas, with his small family. At Bible College he had befriended Luke, and he invited him to come to Gweru with him. Luke was accepted for ordination and he became assistant pastor to Pastor Charles. Pastor Luke married Sarah, they bought a home and settled well in Gweru. When I spent time with them, he told me about his father Ivor. He had recently lost his wife, and was in the depth of depression. Although he had a good farm north of Harare, he had lost the will to live, let alone farm his land. I offered to visit him. Pastor Luke was delighted and soon I travelled the thirty or so miles to Ivor's farm.

Over a cup of tea Ivor told me of his wife's brave battle with cancer. He felt completely lost without her. They had been happily married for over forty years. After listening to his sad story for a considerable time I offered to pray for him. He agreed. I prayed from my heart, and God's presence seemed to descend on us both. Ivor was in tears again, and I knew God had graciously touched his heart. I asked him whether he would also like to be able to pray as freely and confidently as I had just done. Yes, he really wanted that! So I shared the simple and glorious gospel message with him. Before I left I had witnessed the awesome transaction between Saviour and sinner. Ivor was born again! What a triumph! Shortly afterwards Ivor visited Pastor Luke and Sarah in Gweru. Pastor Luke had the wonderful privilege of baptising his own dad. When back at his farm Ivor would travel through to our church in Harare to attend our Sunday service. I would visit him out at the farm.

However, after another visit to Gweru, Ivor stopped coming to our church without any explanation to me. I learned from Penny that he was attending the Rhema Church, as he felt it was "livelier" than ours. I was gutted. Months later Penny phoned me to tell me that Ivor had had a heart attack and was staying with his sister in north Harare. Since the Rhema Church was so large in number, she felt that he would not be visited, even if he were missed. So I visited him there and we renewed our friendship. He was now totally dependent on his sister.

I was in prayer one morning when I felt a strong urge to visit him. I rushed through to our lounge to tell Clare where I was going, and I sped off to Ivor's sister's home, arriving some fifteen minutes later. She showed me through to Ivor's room and left us together. I was there for about five minutes when he had another full-blown heart attack. I leapt from my chair to hold him, and pray for him. He was writhing in pain and it was impossible for me to concentrate on my earnest prayer. Just then his sister returned with our tea. She panicked and rushed for the phone. I overheard her telling his cardiologist that she had finished the injections he had prescribed, and that there was no way she could leave Ivor to collect any more. That was when she remembered I was there. She rushed through to where I was. She asked if I could race down to Second Street to collect the life-saving medication for him. Of course I could! She confirmed it with the cardiologist, gave me the address to go to, and I raced off to collect the injections from a waiting receptionist. I put my hazard lights on, and broke the speed limits there and back. Ivor's sister, a retired nurse, administered the injection, and almost immediately Ivor recovered, and settled. "Praise the Lord you were here!" exclaimed Ivor. I told him and his sister (a not-yet Christian) how that I had felt the strong urge to visit him in a hurry. I was so grateful that I obeyed – and once again I was in awe of a God who knows the future in detail!

Ivor's heart was irreparably damaged. He lived for only a couple more weeks. I do not know why God had extended his life as he had. Perhaps God was reaching out to Ivor's sister? Pastor Charles from Gweru was asked to conduct his funeral at the Warren Hills Crematorium. I attended the funeral and the reception afterwards. It became clear that for some reason Pastor Luke did not acknowledge my involvement in his father's spiritual journey. I felt ignored and unwelcome, so I quietly slipped away without saying much at all.

I too had lost someone with whom I had formed a spiritual bond. I had learned my lesson from Janet's departure, and I never asked for thanks from Pastor Luke or his family.

Ivor came to Christ after hearing my heartfelt prayer for God's comfort after he had told me a very long story of the loss of his wife. I have many stories of my prayers opening doors for the sharing of the Gospel of the Lord Jesus. Here is another:

Within a short time of being in Harare, there was a court-case of the former Air-Vice-Marshall of the Rhodesian Air Force. Henry was being tried, along with five other air-force officers, on trumped-up charges of treason. They had all given statements under torture. After extracting these statements they were committed to the Wha Wha Prison awaiting trial. Whilst there, the Administrator of the air-force whose name was William, had arranged for Pastor Charles to hold communion with them. The Air-Vice-Marshall was challenged by the message of the communion, and before he partook he asked for prayer to become a Christian. He experienced a wonderful conversion to Christ. Knowing this I became very interested in the court case, and I prayed much for justice to prevail, and for God's hand to be seen. I attended the trial a few times.

William's wife, Anne, was a friend of Pastor Bob, and was one who kept her pledge to support Clare and I in the ministry. She told me one day that Henry's wife Joan had been involved in a car accident, and was in hospital. I felt an urge to visit her there. So I found her private ward and asked to speak to her. She had a friend on either side of her bed. All of them seemed distinctly uncomfortable at my intrusion, and I really struggled to communicate my concerns for her, and her husband. The tension increased, so I excused myself and went down the short passage past the en-suite bathroom to the door. As I was turning the handle I felt I heard God reprimanding me for not praying for Joan. Every previous visit to patients in hospital was ended with a request to them for me to pray. Why not now? Such was the urge that I turned around and went back to her and her friends. I felt the anger, especially from the two friends who were forced to abruptly stop what they had begun to say to Joan.

I said, "I must apologise. I always have offered to pray for the patients I visit in hospital. Would you like me to pray for you?"

Joan looked at her friends who gave that shrug of shoulders that said "anything to just get rid of him"! So she said "Yes, OK," and closed her eyes. I silently asked God to help me, and then I prayed from my heart for her, and Henry. After saying "Amen" I thanked her, and quietly left.

After attending another of the court sessions I was confronted by William. He was a big man with an even bigger presence. "Did you pray for Joan in hospital?" he asked in his usual stern tone. I instantly felt afraid. I felt I was in trouble, and I wondered whether Anne was also in trouble for telling me that Joan was in hospital. I told him that I had – and I was about to apologise, saying that Anne had not requested that I visit – when his demeanour softened.

"I thought it must have been you. She described you to me. She told me that she has never been so moved in all her life!"

The QC from Britain made a mockery of the prosecution, and the Judge had no alternative than to acquit the six of all charges. The Zimbabwe government then declared them prohibited immigrants and they were placed on an airplane to the UK. I am quite confident that God also saved Joan by His grace, and that she has been serving Him alongside her husband ever since.

The lesson here is that *"Salvation belongs to our God, who sits on His throne"*. That throne is a throne of grace, and we have the indescribable privilege of boldly approaching Him in "time of need". A sincere heartfelt prayer has the power to convince the not-yet-Christian that God is real, and that He hears and answers prayer. Only the Holy Spirit can convince a sinner of the peril he is in because of his sin, and reveal to him his one and only Saviour, Jesus Christ, who paid in full the penalty for that sin. Prayer is a wonderful way not only of opening heaven, but also of revealing Christ!

There have been people who have left my church because they have had a fall-out with someone else in the fellowship. That is common when it has been a break-up of a relationship. I always find it hard when others in the fellowship ask for the reason for a departure. Even if I know the reason, I have learned to always put as positive a spin on it as I can. I do want to keep my hands open! Rumours are inevitable when anyone leaves. One person leaving may trigger the departures of others. Sometimes I have felt fingers pointing at me! I have learned to weather the storm, maintain my dignity as a minister of the Gospel, and call upon God to heal the gaping wounds in my heart. For a shepherd-at-heart, it is very, very hard to lose even one sheep! We have been very grateful to all our members who have rallied around us during such trials – and we have "felt" their prayers. They have been the Aarons and Hurs who have supported us in the battle and brought about the victories that we have so relished!

It has proved very traumatic for us to leave a pastorate too. By God's grace we have led people to Christ, restored others to Him, and developed the faith of many. To leave them to take up a new pastorate has been followed by a season of grief. I remember well when I announced our departure from Hailsford to our Sunday School superintendent and her worship-leader husband. "I thought that it was the children who were expected to leave home, and not the parents!" she said tearfully. I so wanted to take them with us! Not only were they the most faithful and active members, they also supported us through our trials, blessed us in our triumphs, and enabled us financially to end up buying our very own home in Livingston.

The grief is intense because the former congregation members switch allegiance (and rightfully so) to their new leadership. Most of them no longer communicate with us, and neither do we with them. If the essence of death is separation in terms of no longer being able to communicate, then leaving a pastorate that we had poured our lives into is like the loss suffered by the death of loved-ones.

The lesson is do not leave a pastorate unless you have overwhelming guidance by God to do so. Then allow God's comforting presence to envelop you and empower you for the service to come. In a wonderful sermon I heard from John Glass on "Shaking the dust off your feet", he so ably taught us to not expect the same in the new assignment as we found in the one we had just left. Human nature is similar everywhere we go, but each pastorate has been different. God's grace and wisdom is always sufficient for each assignment, if we are humble enough to avail ourselves of them through prayer.

† CHAPTER 12

Lessons from the Battle to Build Church Buildings

I was delighted at the invitations I received to preach in some of our Shona-speaking churches in Harare. I built good friendships with four Shona pastors, one of them called Pastor Amos. He had been converted through the faithful witness of his Christian boss who had emigrated back to Switzerland when Zimbabwe became independent in 1980. He held church in a classroom at a secondary school in the densely populated township of Chitungwiza.

I encouraged him to look to the Lord for his own church building. That clearly daunted him, and I realised I would need to help practically if that were ever to happen. I had plans drawn up, and I submitted them to the Department of Local Government. The whole of Chitungwiza was built on land belonging to the Government. I was told the wait was up to six months and that I was not to call back before that. I noted when the six months were over and paid the department a visit. I was told that they had a big backlog and that I should call back in a month's time. I kept up these monthly visits for another year.

Eventually the file ended up in the office of an official who was responsible for submitting it to the Government minister for final approval. Then the Zimbabwe Government declared a blanket ban on the use of all their school classrooms. Pastor Amos had no alternative than to gather his church on some public land near his home. This created a real problem because there were no toilet facilities, and the Government health authority hounded them for that. Pastor Amos pleaded with me to speed up the process. I told him all that I had been through already, and asked him whether he could represent his church to this official. Perhaps he had a racial "chip on the shoulder", and I, as a white man, was the hindrance. On the other hand, perhaps he wanted me to pay a bribe to get things moving along.

Pastor Amos was adamant that I would get further than a black man could, and he pleaded with me to keep up the visits. I thought of the importunate widow of Luke 18, and felt my continual pestering would wear the official down and we would finally get the go-ahead. So every two weeks I made the arduous journey to his office in that high-rise office block. Each time he made excuses, and each time he made promises. I prayed and fasted over the matter, as I not only perceived Pastor Amos's frustration, but I also perceived he was not believing me when I told him of my unfruitful visits.

Eventually I saw an opportunity. There had been a lady from Gweru who had been sent to the Pariwenatwa Hospital in Harare for chemotherapy. Her church back in Gweru were praying fervently for her recovery. Her son had risen in the ranks of the post-office, and some envious employees there had told the CIO that he was an illegal immigrant. His dying mother was needed to confirm that he had been born in Zimbabwe but that he had lived most of his growing years in Malawi. She was very keen to be back in Gweru for the court hearing. Well, she died during treatment.

Her family in Gweru were informed and they gathered to discuss fetching her body for burial in Gweru. A death certificate was issued and she was transferred to the morgue. In the morgue she sat up singing a hymn! The morgue attendant took fright and fled! She shouted to him to bring some water as she was thirsty. He returned shortly with a doctor and nurse to find her asking to be allowed to return home to help her son. Arrangements were made, and a nurse accompanied her on the train that evening to Gweru. This story was leaked to the press and they sensationalised it. No doubt the doctor who issued the death certificate, and the other medical staff involved, had to answer some tough questions.

I had noticed that every time I visited the official who held our application file he had the daily newspaper spread out on his desk. I had wondered that all he did in his long day at work was read the newspaper. I was sure he would have read about that lady who had risen from the dead. So I revisited him and asked him whether he had read that story in the paper. Yes, he had. I told him that that true story was the result of prayer. I looked over at his bookshelf to his left and said, "Our file has not moved from where I saw it two weeks ago. I am now going to pray to the God who raised that lady from the dead to punish you for holding up His work in Chitungwisa."

I was surprised at my boldness, but even more surprised at his reaction. He shot out of his chair and half knelt before me as he begged me not to pray that prayer! I told him that I would give him another week to have the file with the Minister of Local Government. He walked me to the lift and as the doors of the lift were closing he was pleading with me not to pray that prayer.

The following Tuesday I was back in his office. He rose from the table to greet me as a long lost friend. He was smiling ear to ear. I knew he had good news for me. Our file was with the minister! I never prayed "that" prayer. I then asked him politely to arrange a meeting between me and the minister. Eager to please, he phoned through straight away. I could tell immediately, by the conversation I heard, that this official really feared his superior. That fear rubbed off on me. He secured a five minute interview and led me meekly down the long corridor to the minister's plush office.

He too had the newspaper spread out on his desk before him. His reception of me was hostile. My immediate thought was that he had been given this post as a reward for his involvement in Mugabe's terror war. His tone revealed that he was boss, and that he did not like the white man! I respectfully told him about my two year quest for land to build a church for the people of Chitungwisa. I told him I was grateful to speak to him, and I asked him for favour in the matter. He promised to consider it, but he was not going to promise a favourable outcome. I thanked him and withdrew.

I spent the whole journey home praying for God to turn the man's hard heart, and for God to secure a victory for His waiting church. Shortly after I returned home I received a phone call from a man telling me that he was a journalist working for the *Sunday Herald*. He told me that he was investigating the difficulties churches were encountering when it came to securing land for church buildings. He made it clear that he was interviewing a number of church leaders on this subject. I told him all the difficulties we had experienced over the past two years, including the closure of classrooms to all churches, and the harassment of open-air meetings by government officials. He asked me whether I believed that the Government was pursuing an anti-Christian agenda. I said an emphatic "yes", and he immediately asked whether I minded being quoted in his article to be published that Sunday. Without even thinking about the possible repercussions, or even shooting up a prayer to God for guidance, I agreed. He thanked me profusely and rung off.

Then real fear descended on me like a heavy blanket. I thought to phone him back but I did not even know his name. So I fell on my knees before God and interceded until the fear lifted, and God gave me His peace. When I later told Clare she was horrified. "John, what have you done? If your name appears in that article we could be visited again by the CIO! And this time they may take you off to Chikerubi (the dreaded maximum security prison where political prisoners are held without trial – just for saying something like I had said!), and what will happen to us?" That is when I lost my peace, and we were both blanketed in fear. That was eased when we prayed together, asking for God's protection and peace. The fear descended on us again when we read the *Sunday Herald* after lunch that Sunday. The only name given in the article was my name. It accurately recorded all that I had told the journalist, including the bit about the anti-Christian agenda of our Government.

It was a real trial we went through as we waited for the CIO to return. They didn't. The next morning the official at the planning office phoned to tell me the good news that we had our land to build our church. He told me that the Minister had read the article in the Sunday paper, and had decided to give us the approval. I feel emotional now as I recall the overwhelming relief for both Clare and I. The Head of the Church had intervened – and won the battle!

I asked to collect the approved plans, I prayed a blessing on the official (to his delight), and I rushed around to the chocolate factory where Pastor Amos worked. His face showed both horror and disbelief at my story as I told him all. He was overwhelmed with emotion as I pointed to each plan that had the coveted stamp of approval. The long wait was over. He gave me a bear-hug and would have kissed me all over if that had been his custom. He warned me that I could still be in trouble, and he assured me of his prayers for my protection. I never did find out who tipped off that journalist – or if indeed it was a genuine enquiry, timed by an all-knowing God who had sovereignly undertaken for us.

That weekend I attended our annual convention at the Gweru Agricultural Showgrounds. As soon as I could I excitedly told Pastor Paul that we had the go-ahead to build a 600 seater church in Chitungwisa. I had saved it to tell him in person. He did not receive the news as I had anticipated. His face hardened as he said, "You are very lucky you know." Immediately I felt that I was in trouble. Had he read the article in the national paper? Did he think I had severely prejudiced the denomination I served?

"Last week I received a letter, from a pastor, formally denouncing you as a racist. A short while ago he came to see me to withdraw the letter. If he had not, you would be facing discipline!"

My jaw must have dropped. This news numbed me! Who on earth would accuse me of being a racist? And why tell me the main content of the letter if that letter had been withdrawn? I looked down at the floor, placed my hands on top of my head, and shook it too and fro. My first thought was that the author of the letter was a member of our Belvedere Shona Service. We had about seventy converts to follow up from the 1985 Reinhard Bonnke crusade in the Harare Showgrounds. Since most of these had Shona as their first language, we decided to start a Shona service in our church on Sunday afternoons.

A Shona-speaking evangelist began the church with most of those converts. Our English service remained multi-racial. However, one of the Shona service members had tackled me on the "segregation" of "blacks from whites". I had explained to him that the services were separated on the basis of language and not race – and that he was very welcome to attend our English service. Perhaps he had sent the letter to Pastor Paul. Pastor Paul must have thought that I did not believe him, so he told me that the author of that letter was Pastor Amos. An overwhelming weakness came over my body. I withdrew quickly so that I could sit down. The knife had found my heart, and it had been twisted.

Perhaps Pastor Amos had written that letter out of sheer frustration at the lack of progress in the approval of the building plans. Worse still, perhaps he had felt that I had been lying about my fortnightly visits to the planning office. When I could eventually think straight I determined that Pastor Amos would never know that I was told about his letter (at the time of writing he would be with the Lord in heaven). I also determined that I would never tell Pastor Paul about the risk I had taken, or indeed any of my story. I did feel that it was very wrong to have told me the content of a withdrawn letter. Even though I placed the matter over and over again into my Advocate's nail-pierced hands, I struggled to enjoy any part of the conference.

I took my wage from the tithe of a doctor who had become a member of our fellowship, and I dedicated as much of the rest of the tithes and offerings as possible to the building of that Chitungwisa church. Pastor Paul had told me that *Christ for all Nations* Bible Institute had a funding scheme for the building of churches in the third world. If we could provide them with photographic proof of a building up to roof height, they would fully fund the cost of the roof. So as soon as Pastor Amos informed me that the last brick had been laid, I rushed out to the site to take photographs. I took the negatives to a photoshop and had them printed out. Then I couriered them off, with a covering letter, to Pastor Paul in Gweru.

About a month later I phoned him to ask if he had been successful in securing funding. He told me that he was traveling to Dallas in two weeks' time and he would be taking the photos in person to the Institute. I politely thanked him. A month later Pastor Paul was back. I phoned him for an update. He told me that the donors wanted three identical photos, and not the three different ones I had sent. Although I found that hard to believe, I calmly promised him three identical photos by courier for the next day. I rushed down to the photoshop with my negatives, and I kept my promise.

About three weeks later the funding came through. Pastor Paul promised me that he would take the plans through to Tor Structures in Kwe Kwe who would fabricate the steel roof trusses and install the roof for us. He promised to see them on that Monday. A week later I heard on the news that the price of steel had doubled. I immediately phoned Pastor Paul to confirm he had beaten the price hike. He told me that he had been busy the previous Monday and would be seeing to the roof within the next couple of days. I was furious, not only because of all the delays, but also at the broken promise. I told him that there was no way that we would fund the extra cost because of his failure to keep his promise. I regretted it afterwards, but for the first time ever I put the phone down without saying goodbye or my customary "God bless you". I do not know how the roof was finally funded. All I know is that before we left Harare the roof was on, the congregation were in, and apart from finishing touches like plastering, that project was complete (not without trials along the way) – to the glory of God.

The building of the church building in the Glenview suburb of Harare was a lot more straightforward. The land was owned by Harare City Council and so politicians were not involved – at least not then. They had certain sites allocated for church buildings. Pastor Alan, a colleague and close friend from another denomination, had secured one site that had clay soil. He had spent half the total budget on piles and reinforced foundations. So when I had surveyed the clay land allotted to our new building, I re-visited the council offices. I told the planning officer about the expense Pastor Alan had incurred with the foundations of his church building, and I insisted on being allocated a site on good ground.

He showed me the map and found what turned out to be a perfect site. God gave us favour, and it was allocated to us. Pastor Paul had somehow secured funding for another church in Harare. We agreed together to lay the foundations and floor, then to erect a "Tor Structure" which meant steel uprights holding steel trusses with a corrugated iron roof. Then all that remained was for the congregation members to build the walls as and when they could afford bricks, and cement. When we left Harare that "house of God" had not been completed.

In one of Prime Minister Winston Churchill's speeches he advised his student audience, "Never, never give up!" I am grateful, not least on behalf of the Christians in Chitungwisa and Glenview, that I never gave up. To advance Christ's kingdom even on the building front is a battlefield. It took persistence, patience and prayer to "soften the enemy". It also involved massive risks, even if unintentionally or naively, and God wonderfully overruled and brought the victory. I was not prepared for the counter-attack that floored me. I knew it would come. That has been the pattern after all.

We had initially contracted with the denomination to serve the church in Hailsford for two years. As the time came for the ending of that contract we entered a very severe personal trial. Clare was offered her teaching position at Gateway Primary School in Harare. Her time there had been the best years of her working life, and the pull to return to that was very strong. We had a four-bedroomed house and a decent car to return to. The head-teacher at Gateway even offered me a teaching post at the newly created secondary school. President Mugabe's brutal land seizure programme had not yet come into force so that Zimbabwe's economy was not in catastrophic decline yet. So you can imagine the torment we went through deciding whether to stay in Hailsford, or return to Zimbabwe.

We both knew that God wanted me in His ministry as a Pastor, so I wrote to Pastor Paul at our Zimbabwe Headquarters to see about returning to our former church there. Eventually he replied that he had heard good news of our ministry in Hailsford, that Pastor William was firmly in place as Pastor in the church in Harare, and that he felt that it would be better all-round if we remained in Hailsford. When we considered that there would be no replacement in the near future for me at the Hailsford Church, and especially when we considered the future prospects for our sons in the UK, we reluctantly decided to remain.

A Zimbabwean was keen now to buy our home in Harare as an investment. Fortunately he had money with a broker in London, and he was able to release the price of our air-tickets to return and pack up our belongings in Harare. Although it was wonderful to see family and friends again, the packing up of furniture and belongings; the disposing of stuff we did not want anymore, and leaving the land of our birth was extremely hard. Only God knows the extent of the trauma we felt. To sweeten the blow to my beloved wife I promised that I would have our small manse enlarged upon our return. The profit made on the sale of our home translated to a meagre £15,000 after paying back our airfares.

Immediately on our return to Hailsford we negotiated with our HQ first to purchase the manse. When that was flatly refused, we asked for an equity share. Our £15,000 would be our deposit. It would mean that our wages would need to significantly improve out of the new money coming into the church from the mortgage we would raise. There was no other way we could see to owning our own home by the time we retired. That too was flatly refused. Ted, who came down from London to negotiate, accused me of being greedy. Sitting in that room were my elders Ivan (who was buying his council home at a third of its value), Barry (who had just purchased a brand-new home after selling his former home), and Ted who was also buying his own home in London. I tried to explain how morally wrong it was for the church to pay me a low wage that made it impossible for me to raise a mortgage even on a bachelor flat, so that the church could purchase a manse for itself. I understood if there is a mortgage-free house that had been bequeathed to the church for use as a manse. I felt that the minister should be allowed to have a choice of where and how to house his family.

"If you leave Hailsford we will need a manse for the next pastor," was the argument Ted stuck to. If I left, and they sold the manse, they could afford to pay the pastor enough for him to either pay rent on a property of his choosing, or, if he came with a deposit, having sold his former home, he could afford to take out a mortgage of his own. The current system meant effectively that the church was purchasing the manse at the pastor's expense. Whenever he leaves he will leave with nothing, and the church will be left with more of the manse. That, I considered, was morally indefensible. Ted would not budge and my elders did not say a word either way. When I later phoned Pastor Bradley who was now General Overseer (and Ted's Pastor), he very firmly told me that the denomination was no longer doing equity share agreements. I tried every way to argue the point but he too would not budge. I fought that battle hard but lost.

At the next executive meeting I asked for permission to extend the manse. I showed them the plans I had had drawn up, and the estimate I had received for the cost. Ted objected. He would not raise the additional borrowing on the mortgage. When all the other members of the executive seemed to side with him I very firmly said, "I have made a promise to my wife that I would extend the manse if we remained at our post in Hailsford. I have £15,000 of our own money from the sale of our home in Harare, and I will use that to keep my promise. No one here will stop me!" The room fell silent. I was well known for my gentle nature. This was the first time that they had witnessed such firmness from me. Then suddenly it was unanimously approved – and Ted promised to raise the extra mortgage! That battle I won, praise the Lord.

I had acquired the service of a young man who had only just completed his apprenticeship, his friend who was an excellent bricklayer, and Jack, the brother of our organist at the church. I helped with the digging of the foundation and other non-skilled work. The extension went up quickly and well within budget and the extra mortgage came through in time to make the last payments, and reimburse Clare and I. When the extension was complete we had the manse valued. It was valued at £102,000. When we were about to leave Horsham twelve years later we had the manse valued again. It was now valued at £330,000.

I then turned my focus to the dilapidated state of the church. It had originally been a Methodist Church. When the attendance dropped to below a viable number the building had been turned into a community centre. Pastor Barry, who founded our church in Hailsford, purchased it at £4,000. I had just read Rick Warren's book *Purpose Driven Church* and in it he stated that you can always tell how a congregation feels about church by looking at the state of the toilets. Ours were a complete embarrassment. So was the back hall to which they were attached. The old kitchen was filled with junk and the make-do replacement at the one end of the back hall was very dilapidated and resting on a very springy rotting wooden floor. So I asked Phil to have plans drawn up for complete renovation, including a mezzanine floor, a Sunday School room upstairs, a new kitchen downstairs with a tiny office above it. And of course new toilets.

I knew from experience that any building project for Christ's church is a battlefield. Having won victories in the past, I was willing, by God's grace, to take on this battle too. The first casualties were two of my elders. They resigned and left the church over my proposed ambitious project. They told me that I was taking too big a risk and they wanted no part in it. Losing them was a terrible blow to me. (One of them had been in the building trade, and had lost everything when the recession hit Britain in the early 1990s. The other was a pessimist by nature. I had worked hard with him to become more positive and trusting. My proposals simply threw him back into pessimism. Shortly after leaving us he was diagnosed with cancer. When we had completed most of our renovations he phoned me to apologise sincerely for letting me down when I needed his support. A week later he went on to be with the Lord.) My current leaders were in their mid to late twenties and were risk-takers themselves. I knew that I had their full and enthusiastic backing.

I appointed Phil as project manager. He could rally volunteers from the church to do what they could, and he, with a team of skilled artisans, could complete the works. The estimated cost was extremely reasonable. So I took the proposed project to the next Executive meeting. Bearing in mind that the previous December we had completely emptied our bank account repairing the church's leaking roof, and that we had already raised additional borrowing for the extension of the manse, Ted told me that I was crazy to take on this project without all the money up front. He said that our current mortgage was all that the church could afford. He predicted financial disaster, with the executive having to pick up the pieces. The other members of the executive voiced that they had grave concerns, with Pastor Bradley saying that he will first need to speak to our leadership about this. He told me that I needed an increase in wage, and that he wanted them to know that their pastor's well-being came first. I insisted that the project was my prayer-soaked idea, that I saw it as an investment in God's Kingdom.

I told the Executive that we had set up a building fund, and that no money for the project would come from the general fund which paid my wages and other church expenses. I announced Clare and I were prepared to loan the church the money we had from the sale of our home in Harare. I also gave testimonies about building two churches back in Harare when we did not have all the money up front. God had provided as we went along, and I was confident He would do the same for this project. Pastor Bradley still insisted on speaking to our leaders (without me being present), and he came away from that meeting saying that he now knew that all the leaders were 100 per cent behind the proposed project. So he cautiously gave us the go-ahead. One good thing about that meeting was that Phil afterwards came to ask me whether I was coping on my wage. I told him that it was a real struggle for us each month. He then secured us a £200 a month increase.

When the back hall, toilets and fully fitted kitchen (including a commercial dishwasher) were complete I gave testimony to God's provision, and blessing, to the Executive. They seemed amazed and gave God thanks too. Then I hit them with the next phase. I wanted to completely renovate the main hall, with a mezzanine floor across that great expanse so that we could effectively double the size of our church building. The plans had already been drawn, and the estimated cost was over £90,000. Once again I was considered irresponsible. Once again I stood my ground. This time I had a fresh testimony of God's provision to reinforce my case. Pastor Bradley once again asked me whether our leadership were fully behind this new project. He believed me this time when I assured him they were. To ease their concerns I discussed the two phases, and that our first concern would be to complete the first phase of a new concrete floor, a mezzanine floor with suspended ceilings and good lighting, and double glazed windows. The second phase of making rooms upstairs would only be worked on once everything was complete, and paid for, downstairs. The amazing story of the provision and blessing of God for this project is also recorded in *Privileged Witness*.

The battle was worth it, not only for the wonderful testimonies of God's timely provisions, but also in the resultant growth of the church of Jesus Christ. A great spin-off to the completion of our project was that Pastor Bradley rallied his leadership around to giving the go-ahead for the wonderful refurbishment and redecoration of his church building in London. One of his members was a builder and he made an excellent job of it.

The counter-attack for the completion of this building project, I believe, was the break-up of Phil's marriage. I devote a chapter to that sad story later in this book.

†CHAPTER 13

Lessons from Blue on Blue or so-called Friendly Fire

One of the first graduates from the Bible College in Gweru was a very bright young man called Pastor Sam. He was a star student, so much so that he was asked to preach at our annual convention. He had also been given a church to pastor in Harare. Although I was impressed by his eloquence and confidence when he preached at that conference, I had a nagging feeling that He was not walking with His Saviour.

A month or so after that sermon I had a phone call from Pastor Paul in Gweru. He told me that Pastor Sam had been accused of fornication with an under-aged girl in his congregation. He wanted me to gather up Pastor Titus, the district minister for Harare, and to bring Pastor Sam down to Gweru to face the charges for possible discipline. So I drove the three hour journey with Pastor Titus in the front and Pastor Sam in the back seat. Pastor Titus and I were great friends so we were able to engage in conversation, much of it about the Lord and His Word.

When we arrived in Gweru we found Pastor Paul had gathered Pastor Charles, Pastor Mark and two local black pastors. Pastor Sam did the sensible thing and admitted to his great sin. He was asked to leave the room whilst we discussed his discipline. When he returned he was given six months suspension from all ministry. Pastor Titus was then asked to oversee his restoration. Then all the black pastors were dismissed and I was asked to remain. I felt a terrible foreboding that I was also in trouble as both Pastor Charles and Pastor Paul seemed tense.

Pastor Paul then told me that my assistant minister Pastor Warrick had been talking to them, and on the grounds of what he had told them, they wanted me to stand down from the ministry. He then offered me the post of science teacher at the Christian Secondary School in Gweru. I felt knifed in the heart! I felt complete disbelief and for a few moments I could not speak. I asked them what Pastor Warrick had said that brought them to this decision, and they told me that they could not disclose that. They were very serious and looked coldly on me for my reply. My reply was that I would first need to bring it before the Lord in prayer. I do not think that they were expecting that response. A very awkward silence fell over us all, and I rose from my chair and left.

I gathered Pastor Titus and Pastor Sam, and began our very long journey home. There was very little conversation in the car. I was in no mood for that. My heart was breaking, and I was driving in the dark, with rain beating on the windscreen, and the wiper blades crossing to and fro. In the light of oncoming headlights Pastor Titus noticed the tears streaming down my cheeks and he asked me whether I was OK. I told him that I was very sad. He did not press me – I guess he felt I was sad about Pastor Sam, and he was too. Pastor Sam was facing six months suspension for fornication with a 15 year old girl, and I was to leave the ministry altogether. I had been twelve years in faithful ministry. I had had no such moral lapses. It had to be more than what Pastor Warrick had said. It had to be something to do with his ambitions. He was the second pastor to want to usurp me. The black pastors held me in esteem. No wonder they were not included in the proceedings. I could not for a moment believe that my accusers were led by the Lord in this matter. Was the Holy Spirit also grieving? I was turning most of my tormenting thoughts into prayer. I was also doing a lot of quiet groaning and sighing (Romans 8:26).

Clare was in bed and asleep when I finally arrived home. So I lay there beside her wondering how she, our sons, our congregation, and friends would react to this news I was finding impossible to cope with. Eventually exhaustion, especially emotional, overwhelmed me and I fell asleep. In the morning I wondered whether it had all been just a bad dream. Clare knew immediately that something was wrong, but she had to get ready for teaching and we agreed to talk about it all when she returned home. I visited Pastor Warrick that morning. A friend and former pastor of his was there too. I told Pastor Warrick in front of Pastor Gavin that on the grounds of what he had been telling Pastor Paul and Pastor Charles, I had been asked to stand down from ministry. Pastor Warrick looked over to Pastor Gavin and broke into a smile that told me that he was pleased with the outcome. He now stood to inherit my church. I felt the full weight of the betrayal, and I withdrew from his home, which was the church manse, before my tears could be seen.

At about 11am I received a phone call from Pastor Paul. He wanted to know my decision. I told him that I had prayed, and I strongly believed that God wanted me to remain in His ministry. He angrily told me that I had no option but to leave the ministry. That is when I felt the knife in my heart had been twisted. I said goodbye and crumpled into the armchair. I began to weep. It was coming from deep in my abdomen. When I was truly exhausted with emotion, I fell quiet. That is when I believe I heard the Lord Jesus speak to my heart. *"Indeed, Satan has asked for you, that he may sift you as wheat. But I have prayed for you, that your faith should not fail,"* (Luke 21:31). I argued in my heart that that word was for Simon Peter, not for me. After a little while it dawned on me that this is a word for so many facing a fierce battle. Then I was quietly thrilled that Jesus had prayed for me. My faith would not fail!

At about 12 noon a good friend of ours called to drop something at our home. She looked at me with my bloodshot eyes and she exclaimed, "What on earth has happened to you?" At our front gate I poured out the whole story to her. She was horrified to the point of panic. She then told me what happened to her pastor. She had been his personal assistant. He pastored a wonderful church in Harare, oversaw a wide range of mission stations, and he was on the curriculum board for Zimbabwe Education, ensuring Christianity was the principle religion studied in schools throughout Zimbabwe. We all held him in high esteem, yet a minister under him had been complaining about him to his mission board in the UK. They sent out two ministers to "resolve the issue". Her pastor first knew something was terribly wrong when these two refused to stay with him as at previous visits. They hired a car, booked into a hotel and visited him very formally.

The betrayal almost instantly robbed him of his good health. Within weeks he was diagnosed with inoperable and terminal cancer, and within weeks of the diagnosis he was with His Saviour in heaven! She was petrified that the same may happen to me.

Clare was absolutely wonderful when she arrived back from her teaching at lunchtime. She listened to both my story and I told her our friend's story. She calmly reassured me, and loved me. She believed that God still wanted us in His ministry, only not with our current leadership. And as with so many times before, she was led by the Lord, and she was right. We chose not to tell a soul, not even our sons. We knew Pastor Thomas and his wife Rachel were coming to Harare at the weekend, and we would hold off doing anything until we had received their counsel. He had been our Pastor in Bulawayo and had conducted our wedding service. They walked close with the Lord for decades, and were deeply spiritual and calmly wise.

The next morning, the 11th August, 1992, I received a phone call from Rachel. She firstly told me that she and Pastor Thomas had come three days early to stay with their son in Harare. She announced that she had been woken up in the middle of the night with a very clear word from God for Clare and I. This had never ever happened to her before in all the years she had known the Lord. She wanted to know when Clare would be home from work, and she invited herself (and Pastor Thomas) to visit us in the afternoon. She had written the prophecy down, and as soon as she could she read it out to us. Here it is in full:

"John – you of all men – have always known of my love for you. Keep this truth always before you, in the forefront of your thinking. Your strength, your hope, your success lie in the Lord, and are not in any man. Learn to depend only on Me, and not on the support of any other person. Your success is measured by what I see – and have seen – in your heart, and not by what is seen by man, or perceived by you yourself. Acquaint yourself continually, more and more, with the whole counsel of God: and with constantly renewed mind and with your whole heart seek to <u>do</u> it, and teach others also. As you and Clare lift up your heads, and square your shoulders, and face the challenges with confidence in <u>Me</u>, you will find yourself walking in the power, and joy, and comfort of the Holy Spirit."

If you are going through a similar trial right now, please accept this prophecy for yourself!

Every word carried deep meaning to Clare and I. We both became very emotional and tears flowed freely in front of our precious guests. Then almost together Pastor Thomas and Rachel gently demanded to know what was going on. We told them. They expressed their horror and disgust and promised that they would be doing more than praying about it. Clare and I not only marvelled at God's timing (Pastor Thomas and Rachel came three days before expected), but particularly the accuracy of every word of her prophecy. Our Father in heaven had answered the prayer of His beloved Son, *"Holy Father, keep through Your name those whom You have given Me, that they may be one as We are."* The NASB says, *"Holy Father, keep them through the Name which You have given Me."* (John 17:11b) and again in verse 15, *"I do not pray that You should take them out of the world, but that You should keep them from the evil one."*

So we lifted up our heads, squared our shoulders, and faced the challenges to come. That Sunday Clare played the keyboard as usual, I preached as usual, and none in the congregation had any idea of what that week had brought us. However, at the end of the service I looked over to the back of the church. Rachel, who was about five feet tall and of small frame, had Pastor Warrick up against the wall. He was six feet tall and at least twice her weight. She had her index finger waving under his nose. I, to this day, do not know what she said to him. What I do know is that he came to visit us that afternoon. I believe that he had seen the evil of his way, and he wanted to fully repent towards us. He then offered to stand down from being my assistant. I accepted both his repentance and offer.

We prayed together, and he left. Pastor Thomas had phoned Pastor Paul to express his feelings about the matter, and Pastor Paul arranged a meeting the following week in a town half-way between Harare and Gweru. Clare and I arrived at the hotel to be met by a room full of white pastors. Clare had asked me if she could do most of the talking. She did so with elegance, grace and profound wisdom. She spoke of my diligence to serve the Lord out of love for Him, His Word, and His people. She disclosed some of the hidden things she knew that had not been known by any of those present. When someone tried to say something she politely asked if she could finish first. When she did finish, Pastor Charles assured her that they had given me an option to stay or leave. Pastor Paul had the opportunity to correct that but chose to remain silent. Then there was a chorus affirming us and our ministry and backing off the original intention. I was in awe of the lady God had chosen to walk alongside me! I felt God's pleasure with her.

Since this was the second time we had been betrayed by our leaders, Clare and I looked for new leaders. We phoned Ted in London and asked whether there was the possibility to "pulpit swap" with a minister from the UK. He told me that that seemed unlikely as there was a chronic shortage of ministers in the UK. He promised to discuss my request with the executive and a month later we received a phone call from London. Ted asked me to consider prayerfully a call to pastor a church in Hailsford. The pastor had left "in the dead of the night", and now the lead elder had also left. Ted feared that the church would collapse, and be forced to close. The executive in London had unanimously agreed to ask me to rescue it for them.

After prayer Clare and I agreed to move to Hailsford for two years. It would be an "adventure" for the whole family. A couple of weeks before we left Harare, I received a wonderful phone call from Pastor Charles. He had listened to my half-hour Sunday service on *Radio One*, and he wanted me to know how much he had appreciated it. For over five years I had been preaching on National Radio – every week at 10am or 12 noon for five minute slots, and once a month for a half-hour slot broadcast on the Lord's Day. This was the first time he had made any positive comment. It made me realise just how much I had wanted his affirmation in the thirteen years I had been a pastor in Zimbabwe. I was very grateful for it, even though God had told me through Rachel, *"Learn to depend only on Me, and not on the support of any other person. Your success is measured by what I see – and have seen – in your heart, and not by what is seen by man, or perceived by you yourself."*

In hindsight I am grateful that Pastor Charles' lack of support and mentoring had contributed greatly to us depending on God. The lesson learned is to seek only God's commendation. He wants to meet my core needs for security, self-esteem and significance. If I receive His "Well done, good and faithful servant", it will not matter at all whether I am praised, ignored or denounced by any other person.

About four years later I heard that Pastor Paul was visiting Pastor Bradley in London. So I phoned and asked if I could speak to him. I asked him all about himself, his family, and folk we both knew back in Zimbabwe. I believe he detected no bitterness in my tone or voice. Long before I had placed the entire charge sheet in the Lord Jesus' hands, just as I had been taught by God near the beginning of my ministry. Later Pastor Bradley told me how very blessed Pastor

Paul had been with my phone call. I think that it was because he had believed that I would never want to talk with him again. So ended a very severe trial.

✝ CHAPTER 14

Lessons from Dealing with a Divisive Man

The church we came to in Hailsford was in crisis. The numbers had dwindled to about twenty-four adults. Many of them told me that they had hung on to see what Clare and I were like. They had been on the point of leaving too. I was told that there was a faction of about eight members who were very against our coming. They had not been consulted, and had been given no choice! They also had a super-spiritual notion that the Holy Spirit was to be their pastor – and not someone imposed on them "by man".

The "leader" of this faction was Robert, the son of Byron and Gwen. We met him whilst staying with his parents prior to moving into the manse. We said hello to him and extended our hands to shake his, but he looked straight past us to talk with his mother. She looked embarrassed at his lack of common courtesy and later defensively informed us of his annoyance that we were being "imposed on the church without any consultation".

Many years later I met with the previous pastor who had left suddenly. One week he was at church, and the next he was gone! He congratulated me on turning things around. He told me he felt that there had been an undercurrent of discontent that he could not pin down or understand. Someone was leading this rebellion but he could not tell who. That was one of the big reasons for his "flight". I told him that by the time we arrived the leader of the rebellion was very obvious. That had made it so much easier for me to tackle. This was to be confirmed by Phil and his wife Joy. They came to greet us in the manse shortly after we had moved in. Phil played the keyboard and Joy led the vocals. They told me that if Robert disapproved of a song that they had chosen to sing in church, he would simply sit down and that would be the cue for seven others to sit out the song with him. That made it very difficult for them to lead worship. I assured them that I would tackle this rebellion as soon as I had gathered enough first-hand evidence myself. They promised to pray for God to give me wisdom, and I assured them that I would be praying for the same.

It was whilst praying for the church with its crisis that I read Titus 3:9–11, *"But avoid foolish disputes, genealogies, contentions, and strivings about the law; for they are unprofitable and useless. Reject a divisive man after the first and second admonition, knowing that such a person is warped and sinning, being self-condemned."*

I took this as the procedure the Holy Spirit wanted me to carry out. I prayed earnestly that He would give me the wisdom and opportunity to do so to the glory of God, and the saving of that little church.

On our first Sunday Pastor Barry (the general overseer of the group of churches) was present to induct Clare and I into the pastorate. The rebellious group were not present because, as I was to learn later, they had no time or respect for Pastor Barry. Those who were there were thrilled to have us and made us feel very welcome.

The following Sunday we had our first real test with the rebels. Phil and Joy, with Stuart on the drums, were leading us in the song *More Love, More Power* when I noticed Robert sitting back into his chair, throwing his shoulders back and folding his arms. The others in "his" group then followed his lead. I could see immediately how this affected the worship group, who tried in vain to "pump up" the song. As soon as they finished, Robert stood to his feet and with a strong voice said, "Hear the word of the Lord! There is the spirit of the anti-

Christ in your midst, and the song you have just been singing has been addressed to the spirit of Simeramus! I call on thee to repent, says the Lord Almighty!"

I could not believe what I was hearing! I shot to my feet and said, "That so-called prophecy was not from the Lord! We will start the service again from scratch, and I will be having a word with Robert after the service!" To my surprise Robert and his group remained in the meeting. Soon we were back in a good place for me to preach my first sermon. I preached about the pre-eminence of Jesus Christ – that the Gospel or Good News comes in the person of Jesus Christ and that He was to be the reason for our living on this earth. The church was His and He is her Head! However we are, and whatever we do, we must give Him the pre-eminence!

The "good group" were very grateful to me for the sermon and the way I had handled the "disruption". Phil was able to say, "Now you see what we have been up against." I told him and Joy that our eyes must always be fixed on the Lord Jesus, that we are worshipping Him and not pleasing man. I told them that I felt that they had done a great job leading us in worship – and especially that they had recovered very well after the disruption! I then turned to Robert who was waiting impatiently to speak with me.

"What was wrong with my prophecy?" he demanded.

"There are tests for prophecy in the Bible," I began, "First it must line up with the written Word of Scripture. Second, it must be in line with the revealed character of God. And third, it must edify, exhort and comfort the church. In my judgement, your prophecy fell down on every one of those points."

Robert's face flushed with anger at my reply. "Who made you to be a judge over me?" he sputtered. "What was not Scriptural in my prophecy?" By now, some of his group were moving closer to come to his defence. He had probably told them at the beginning that he could handle his confrontation with me alone. Now they saw he was angry, they wanted to lend him their support. He looked at them and moved his head to indicate that he did not need their support.

"The Holy Spirit, and not the spirit of anti-Christ, was in this place," I said with confidence. "Please tell me about the 'spirit of Simeramus'," I asked.

"The spirit of Simeramus," he confidently retorted, "is spoken of in the Book of Ezekiel!"

"I have never read about that spirit, and I have read through the Bible many, many times," was my answer. "Please show me the Scripture you are referring to."

Robert fumbled in his Bible for a few moments and then told me that he would look it up in his concordance when he returned home, and phone me with the reference. I then asked him, "Where in the Bible is a spirit ever given a 'proper name' – like 'Simeramus'?"

Robert brightened up as he felt he would now outwit me. "There is the name 'Legion' in the New Testament – remember? The one Jesus cast out of the maniac of Gadara!" His tone had turned decidedly sarcastic.

"Please tell me why he called himself Legion?" I asked calmly.

Robert paused as he thought carefully how to answer. Then he said quietly, "I suppose because it says 'for we are many'."

"Exactly!" I replied. "Now I consider your sitting down for that song, and the subsequent prophecy, as divisive. I warn you now that I will not be tolerating that in this church over which Jesus Christ has appointed me as His under-shepherd."

When Robert left me to join with his group I knew that my troubles with them were not yet over.

During the week that followed Byron came to see me. After the pleasantries he asked me to call a church meeting. I asked him what he meant. "We need to discuss the way you handled things on Sunday – there has been quite a bit of discontent about that. Also we need to know what your 'vision' is for the church, and what we can expect for the future direction of this church," was his reply. Then he added, "That's the way issues are tackled here in the UK." He probably suspected, based on the way I had asked the question, that holding a 'church meeting' was not the way we handled issues back in Zimbabwe.

I then asked him how the meeting would run, and told him that although I was not happy with that I would "give it a go" because he had asked for it. That Sunday I announced the date and time for the church meeting. I added that if anyone had an issue with me, the clear instruction of Matthew 18:15–18 is that they must first speak to me alone. If I did not "hear" them then they were to "bring a witness". If that does not reconcile matters then, and only then, they could bring the matter before the church. I invited anyone with a grievance to see me after the church service.

The only one to see me after the service was Robert. My sermon had been on *Leadership in the Bible*. He told me that he did not agree with a single thing that I had preached. I then handed him my notes, saying, "I would like you to go through my sermon. I have written it all out, including the Scripture verses. You will find that I have used over thirty Scriptures on leadership in the church. I will give you all the time you need to come back to me with all the Scriptures you disagree with and why you do. And by the way," I added, "do you have the Scripture reference for 'the spirit of Simeramus'?"

"No," he replied as he took my sermon notes. "But it is to be found in Jewish fables relating to the time of the captivity of the Jews in Babylon."

"Robert! Have you not read Paul's command to Titus to 'not give heed to Jewish fables'?" was my reply, to which he had no answer.

That afternoon Phil and Joy visited us at the manse. They warned me that I was in for a rough time at the 'church meeting'. "They put the pastor in the dock and they attack him from all sides," they continued. They so loathed these meetings that they would not attend themselves – but they would pray earnestly for me to have wisdom and courage to face the critics down. When they left I wondered how many others belonging to the "good group" would be there to support me.

The day of the meeting I set myself to pray and fast. Before the meeting began I prayed with Byron in the vestry. I told him how very uncomfortable I was with what seemed to me to be an unscriptural meeting. He assured me that if I had done nothing wrong then I'd have nothing to be afraid of. "Just explain your words and actions – and your vision. You could appease the critics and even win them over. This meeting is part of being democratic, of making everyone feel they have a part, and a say."

"Christ's church is a 'Theocracy' and not a 'democracy'," I protested as we left the vestry to convene the meeting. The "Robert's group" were all present, and all sitting on my left. They almost outnumbered the others who came. Many of the others were boycotting the meeting. My silent prayer was that they were praying for me. Clare was at home with our sons. I knew she would be praying for me.

My tack was to explain the vision I had for the church. We were starting small, but as Jonathan said to his armour-bearer *"nothing restrains the LORD from saving by many or by few."* I envisioned the church growing to love God more and more, to love one another more and more, to love our neighbour more and more, and to fulfil Christ's great commission to spread the Gospel of Jesus Christ to anyone willing to hear it. How we go about reaching these goals will be to humbly wait on God as our source, inspiration and enabler. I wanted us to stick as close to the New Testament model of church as we possibly could. For all of us it would be a learning process, and an adventure with Jesus, our Lord and Saviour.

I could sense, as I conversed, that there was a growing impatience amongst Robert's group. They wanted to air their grievances, rather than listen to another sermon. I concluded that I had asked the previous Sunday that if any had an issue with me that they spoke to me alone after the service, in accordance with proceedings laid down in Matthew 18:15–17. I said that I was relieved to inform them that only one had done so and that I was addressing his issue with him. There was a sudden uproar from Robert's group. They all had the same issue and wanted it addressed. One shouted, "This is how we do things here in Britain!"

"We must at all costs conduct our affairs as clearly laid down in Scripture," I retorted. "I am not for Zimbabwe culture or for British culture – I am for Christian Culture! You have had your chance and you did not take it. I will not be put in the dock or subject myself to a grilling by any group that is not happy with me or with the way I do things. I am now closing this meeting. We shall never again have such a meeting whilst God has me here as pastor."

Robert's group were not happy! They huddled together in serious conversation. Then they slipped past me to the door without saying a word. Charles and Stacy from the other group came and thanked me for the way I had conducted the meeting. They expressed their great relief that I had called an end to "such awful meetings". They told me that they wondered at how other pastors had survived. They told me that they were sure that those not present would be equally relieved. "We have turned a corner at last!" was their closing comment.

I was relieved that the meeting was now over, and that I had been enabled by the Holy Spirit to be so calm and firm. However I also knew that the battle for the church was not yet over. More was to come.

That Sunday I took as my text *"Or do you think that the Scripture says in vain, 'The Spirit who dwells in us yearns jealously'?"* (James 4:5). I explained that the best definition I had read for jealousy in relation to God's jealousy was "a zeal to protect what to you is very precious". I took the congregation to Scriptures like Exodus 20:5; 34:14; Deuteronomy 4:24; 5:9; 6:15; Joshua 24:19; Ezekiel 39:25 and Nahum 1:2 that describe God as being a jealous God. Exodus 34:14 even tells us that God's name is *Jealous!*

God's "zeal to protect what to Him is very precious" ultimately took Him to Calvary's Cross for our redemption. Yes, believe it or not, we are the objects of His unfailing and limitless love. We are very precious to Him, and He wants us all to Himself! The Holy Spirit who dwells in us yearns for all of us. That is when God's kingdom comes. That is when God's will is done. The last verse I quoted was 2 Corinthians 11:2 *"For I am jealous for you with godly jealousy. For I have betrothed you to one husband, that I may present you as a chaste virgin to Christ."* I urged, in conclusion, for all present to give their all, as living sacrifices, to God and His cause.

That sermon was followed by communion around the Lord's Table. I had introduced matzos (unleavened bread) to represent Christ's sinless body that was broken for us, and non-alcoholic wine to represent the sinless blood of Christ that was poured out for us. In my pre-amble to administering the communion I explained the changes. After the service I was approached by Robert again. I thought maybe he had his answers to my question on leadership in the Bible. "No," he told me, "I am still working on a reply to that. What I am now very angry with is your introduction of sacrimentalism to this church!"

"Sacrimentalism?" I exclaimed, "What do you mean?"

"Don't you know what sacrimentalism means?" he retorted. I shook my head. "You have turned the communion into a sacrifice!" he said angrily.

"I have done no such thing!" I replied. "The bread and the wine are *emblems* of the body and blood of Jesus Christ. I made that clear. By changing them to unleavened versions all I have done is increase the symbolism. I also made that clear. I have NOT turned them into the literal body and blood of Christ!"

Robert did not answer me even though his body language seemed to tell me that I had not won him over. So I warned him again, "Robert, I believe that you are continuing to be divisive. Please stop finding fault!"

As we parted I knew that the time had come for me to carry out the clear instruction of Titus 3:10. I had now warned him twice about being divisive. On both occasions he had not contested that judgment. So when his father phoned me to ask for a meeting with Robert "and a number of others who felt like him", I agreed. No one else was going to be present. It would not be like a church meeting which I had banned. It would also take place in the manse, and not the church.

I prayed and fasted for what I now firmly believed God wanted me to do. Byron came, as did Robert and most of his group. I told them at the start that I was ready to hear their grievances now. I was told that they had not been consulted before my appointment and they did not take kindly to that. They assured me that it was not personal and that anyone imposed on them would have faced the same objection. I acknowledged that and that seemed to embolden them to face me down for being "dictatorial".

They believed Robert's prophecy was definitely from God and I had no right to censure it and so *"quench the Holy Spirit"*. They said that as a matter of fact, and not as a question, so I did not answer them. They then told me that they believed that the Holy Spirit was their pastor and they would therefore not be subject to any man, no matter how godly he may be. I thought that they were becoming unnerved by my lack of defence (God had taught me the power of turning the other cheek!). They had come for a fight and I was not reciprocating. Finally Robert spoke up. He again accused me of introducing sacrimentalism into the church.

He had lit the fuse and I exploded. I opened my Bible at Titus 3 and I read out verse 10. I then told him that I had warned him twice that he was being divisive, each charge he had not contested, and that now I was asking him to leave the church. The others erupted! "You cannot be serious!" "If Robert leaves we will leave with him!" "Have you lost your mind?" were some of the outbursts. What was so surprising to me was the fact that none of Robert's supporters disputed the charge of divisiveness. I guess it was obvious to them. One of them, a school teacher, approached me on the following Sunday to say that he had read Titus 3:10 in the *King James Authorised Version*, and the word used was a "heretic", and not "a divisive man". He then proceeded to tell me sternly that Robert was not a heretic. I calmly told him that the New King James Version translated it as "a divisive man". Surprisingly he still did not contest my judgement that Robert had been divisive!

Soon enough they knew that I was serious and would not

back down. So the meeting came to an abrupt end, and all left for home. Only Byron remained. He told me that he remembered well my sermon on jealousy being "a zeal to protect what to us is very precious". Robert was his son, and although he went about things in sometimes unwise ways, he held to many of the beliefs of his father. "I respect you are a man of the Bible, and I had hoped you and Robert would get along. I am sorry to do this to you so early in your time here in Hailsford, but I do have a zeal to protect my precious son, so I have no choice but to resign my eldership with immediate effect." To my surprise he also did not contest the grounds I had used for Robert's dismissal from our church.

This had been the first time I had ever asked someone to leave the church. I felt completely drained by the "Gethsemane" experience. By that I mean praying in agony to God, *"O My Father, if it is possible, let this cup pass from Me; nevertheless, not as I will, but as You will."* I had a real love and respect for Byron, and his wife Gwen was a real saint. Sleep that night eluded me as I relived all my dealings with Robert and Byron and our new assignment. And yet I sensed God's pleasure and peace in me. This would be a new beginning in the church. The few would become fewer. But there would still be no restraint with God! The Chief Shepherd would yet build His church.

That Sunday Robert brought his wife and children to church. He told me as he entered the church that he was there to say farewell to the church, and that he would not cause me any further trouble. I thanked him and told him that I would make a brief announcement at the end of the service. I also asked Byron if it would be in order for me to announce his decision too. He assured me that he had prayed over it and still felt that it was the right move for him. So at the end of the service I simply said, "It is with sincere regret that I must announce that this is the last service Robert and his family will be attending. We pray God's blessing on them as they seek His will for their future. It is also with sincere regret that I must announce that Byron has stepped down from his role as elder." I looked over to Byron and continued, "On behalf of all the church I thank you for your service as elder to this fellowship. I pray God's rich blessing on you for your future too."

During my sermon that day I had told the famous story of the young boy who had accidentally fallen onto the gears of the railway drawbridge over the Mississippi River. His father had the agonising decision to make – save his son by not lowering the drawbridge – or lower the bridge and so save the four hundred or so passengers on the speeding express train that was hurtling towards him. He chose the latter, and not a soul on board the train knew the price he paid for their safety. As I finished that story, a middle-aged lady, who was one of Robert's group, blurted out loudly, "Oh for goodness sake!"

A short time after the service I asked her whether I could have a private word with her. I took her to the vestry and asked about the outburst during my sermon. "I just cannot stand sentimental, soppy stories," she replied. Then she added, "I suppose now you are going to ask me to leave *your* church!"

"No! I was not going to ask you to leave. I was going to ask you not to embarrass yourself like you did in the service."

"Well my husband and I have decided to leave this church anyway!" she said as she made for the open door.

"God bless you both," I called after her. She turned her head to scowl at me, and she was gone. All of Robert's group left that Sunday. It was really hard for Clare and I. Yet we were abundantly rewarded by those who stayed. We were suddenly their heroes, although we saw no gloating from any of them. Rather there was visible relief.

A few weeks after our "split" one of Robert's group, a young New Zealander called Neville, returned to see me. He apologised for the hard time I had received from the group, and asked whether he could return to our fellowship. He then said, "I have worked out the difference between you and Robert. He seems to see the devil and demons everywhere. He was a soldier, you know, and well, his whole focus seems to be spiritual warfare. You, on the other hand, seem to see God everywhere and your focus is definitely Jesus. I want that!" Neville became a huge blessing to us. After a couple of years he emigrated to the USA to train to be an aircraft technician with Mission Aviation Fellowship. There he met and married a lovely American girl who kept up a correspondence with us for years as they took up different postings with MAF around the world.

News quickly spread to former members and the following Sunday our numbers had swollen to more than what they were before. The whole atmosphere of the church services changed and a new excitement and commitment to serve the Lord Jesus and walk with Him resulted. My first Bible Studies were on personal evangelism – how to lead someone into a relationship with Jesus Christ. We wanted Christ to grow His church through evangelism. We also wanted to win back some of the former members who were not attending any church anymore.

The lessons I learned were to prayerfully obey the clear instruction of Scripture – in this case Titus 3:10 – no matter how hard. The Lord Jesus made this promise in John 12:26, *"If anyone serves Me, let him follow Me; and where I am, there My servant will be also. If anyone serves Me, him My Father will honour."*

God really did honour me for the tough decisions I made. I learned that I must feel secure in God's calling and appointment. He had called me to Hailsford, regardless of the opinions of a few. If I had not firmly believed that, and if I had not called on God for His wisdom, grace and calm boldness, that little church would not have survived the battle for its very life. God had placed me "between a rock and a hard place". I had no money to return my family to Zimbabwe, and I had no prospect of finding employment in that time of recession in the UK. He was with us "in the burning fiery furnace", and He brought us through into sweet victory.

†CHAPTER 15

When the 'Unthinkable' Happens

Kim was just fourteen years old when she first came to our church. Two girls her age had befriended her at school and encouraged her to come. Clare was running the youth at the time and Kim came to the youth too. She later brought her father Jim to our Sunday service. God gave me the huge privilege of leading him into a personal relationship with Jesus Christ. At about the same time Jeff, a man in his mid to late thirties, also came to our church. He ran a photographic studio, specialising in portraits, weddings and other occasions. He was welcomed into the church, and I visited him at his studio a couple of times. He told me that his wife was not interested in church, and would not welcome me into their home.

Every year the Hailsford District Council would run a summer event in the park called the Hailsford Festival. In our first year in Hailsford the King's Church had a special presentation of "The Universe" in a large marquee. It was an excellent production that required a lot of effort. When they discovered that our church was also very keen on outreach they asked us to put on a show for the next festival. We decided to target children at our first Hailsford Festival outreach. So we invited all the Hailsford churches not only to participate, but also to advertise their Sunday School, Youth Clubs, Moms' and Toddlers' Groups and summer activities. The King's Church marquee became a hive of activity. That went down so well that we continued on this theme year after year until Hailsford District Council withdrew the event.

It was at this event that Jeff took a number of photographs of Kim. She was well developed for her age, and that day wore very little clothing. I believe he began to flirt with her. I think that she initially enjoyed the attention but soon felt unnerved. So she let me know what had happened, including her feeling that he had been flirting with her. The following day, after our Sunday morning service, I asked Jeff to join me and Ivan in my little vestry. Jeff went quite pale when I confronted him with what I had been told, and especially when I announced that Kim was only fourteen years old. He told us that he had really believed her to be at least sixteen, if not seventeen years old. Since both Ivan and I could quite easily see how he could be mistaken on her actual age, we took the tack that he was a married man and therefore was completely out of order to flirt with any other female, let alone a teenager. We warned him that should she complain again about any advance from him then we would report him to the police. I never saw Jeff again, and I thought that that was the end of the matter. We did tell Kim about our warnings to Jeff, and said that should he make her feel uneasy again in any way, she must let us know. We would then take it to the police.

In the week that followed I arranged to see Kim's parents. I soon found out that I knew more than they did. They were understandably incensed. I found it very difficult to address the problem of Kim's clothing. I told them that if she was to dress like that in public places, she was bound to attract the attention of perverts and paedophiles. They sheepishly admitted that I could be right, and then told me that Kim was very strong-willed. She would not have them tell her what to wear, or what not to wear. I then told them that if they wanted to press charges against Jeff, that I would fully back them. They promised to think about it. They never pressed charges, and I thought that that was it.

The episode with Jeff made me very vigilant concerning other men in our church. When I thought that there was a friendship between Terry and Kim I called him into the vestry too. He was a bachelor, about twenty five years old, and was simply a fun-loving person who attracted the affection of many of our teenagers. I asked him whether he could be accused of inappropriate behaviour towards under-age girls, with a special mention of Kim. I told him that nothing had been reported to me yet so I had only a hunch something could be going on that could at least be perceived as inappropriate. He seemed most offended and vehemently denied inappropriate behaviour. I assured him that I believed him, but that he must show discretion towards young girls. Maybe I handled it unwisely, but he thought that I thought that he was a paedophile. I found out his thoughts when he told a new teenager not to talk to him, because "the leadership believed him to be a paedophile". She then asked me about it. Terry also left our church.

Not long after that Kim announced to her friends that she was leaving the church. A week later her father tearfully announced that he was also leaving our church. When asked why, he told me that Kim had threatened suicide if he did not. As that was a bitter blow to me, I wondered when this trial would end.

A few months later I had a visit from police officers. They told me that Kim was receiving treatment at a private clinic for anorexia. She had disclosed to her psychiatrist that it all began with Jeff's advances. Her psychiatrist then contacted the police, and they not only wanted a statement from me, but they also wanted me to explain why I had not reported Jeff to them at the outset. It was a terrible experience for me. I apologised profusely and told them all I knew, and all that I had done (including my conversation with Kim's parents). They softened their tone then, but asked me to never again deal with these matters "in-house". I promised them to comply, they left, and I did not hear from them again. I was very relieved that no mention was made of Terry.

Not long after all these events we returned home from church one Sunday to find a hate message spray-painted on our driveway. It took me ages to remove that. We also had two pizza deliveries which we had never ordered, and large bubble wrap envelopes filled with waste food (probably pizza), which we did not open. To this day we do not know who was responsible.

In the year 2000 the census results were published. To my great surprise it showed that 76 per cent of the adult population in our county professed that their religion was Christian. I felt led to write to our local paper about this statistic. My plea was for the media and the general public to take note that every time the name of Jesus Christ is used as an expletive, most of the readers, viewers or listeners will be offended. The editor placed my letter immediately below his comment. In that comment he attacked the "yobs" who had burned down the score-board at the Hailsford Cricket Club. He pleaded with his readers to return to the morals and values once held dear, and he referred to my letter. He closed with an appeal to the churches in Hailsford to come forward with a profile of their activities in the community.

The following week one of the paper's journalists phoned me. He wanted our church to be the first to do a profile for his paper. I arranged a time, and when he arrived with pen and paper I presented him with a written profile. We went through it together and he used most of what I had written. I did encourage him that if the profile put the church in a good light, the rest of the churches in Hailsford would also fully co-operate. That Sunday the paper's photographer arrived to take photographs. The following Friday there was a full page spread all about our church. It was very positive. Sure enough, many other churches were later featured in excellent profiles.

However, whenever something good happens to promote Christ's Kingdom, there is a counter-offensive. Mine was very personal. Another journalist phoned me to say that the paper had been tipped off about a website that had been set up in Clare's and my name. She had been asked by her editor to investigate, with a view to writing a story about it for the paper. I told her that we did not know how to even set up a website so someone else must have been responsible. She told me the web address, advised me to look at it with my wife, and that she had better come and see me soon.

Clare and I were horrified at the content of the website. The picture of us was obviously taken from the newspaper article on our church profile. The contents spoke of us loving paedophiles and perverts. "We welcomed them to take full advantage of our lovely vulnerable teenage girls." The grammar was appalling, but the content was stomach-churning. So was the prospect of a newspaper article on it! The journalist was visibly disturbed when she visited me in my office. She could see straight away that the website was a frame-up. She had never come across such a travesty in all her time as a journalist, I told her that we knew who was the most likely culprit, and she strongly advised me to go to the police to file charges. Very soon into my time with her she promised that there was no way anyone could persuade her to run an article about this website and she advised us strongly to find out the web-master, explain the fraud, and ask for an immediate removal. She phoned me later to say that her editor, having heard her out, was also of the strong opinion to not run a story at all.

Clare managed to contact the web-master and have the website removed. Then we visited the police station. I was very surprised at how uninterested the police were in our case. When I told the lady police officer that we had no intention of filing charges against Kim she suddenly became interested. So I gave her Kim's contact details. I just wanted Kim to be warned so that there was no repeat. The next day that officer phoned to tell me that she had visited Kim. Kim had broken down in tears, admitting her guilt, and promising never again to harass us. I felt a huge weight lift off me, and thanked the officer for a job well done. Clare too shared my relief when I told her the good news.

But that was not the end. Years later Clare was shopping in a bargain store. To her surprise, Kim was on the checkout that Clare had joined. When Clare's turn to be served came, she very graciously greeted Kim. However Kim stiffened, and then very sternly told Clare that she had the right to refuse to serve any customer and she announced that she refused to serve Clare. Clare had never had that treatment in a store before, but so as not to create more of a scene, she meekly gathered her merchandise back into her basket, asked the next customer to excuse her, and she joined the next long queue.

The next day we received a first class letter in the post from the store manager. In it we were told that we were banned from the store, and that if we should enter the store we would be apprehended by their security, the police would be called, and we would be charged. I remember well the mileage that was made by members of the ministers' fraternal after I told them the story. They found it both incredible and hilarious! A new minister came to the next fraternal, and I was introduced to him as the pastor who was banned from shopping at the bargain store! Clare consoled herself that at least we were not banned from Marks & Spencer or Waitrose. We wrote to the manager asking for the reasons for our ban. She told us that she did not have to give a reason. A couple of months later we received a letter from her saying that the employee who had filed a complaint against us had left their employment, and that we were now free to return to shop with them. She did not disclose Kim's complaint. We never did return to shop there.

The great lesson is to have a good safeguarding policy, safeguarding co-ordinators, and vigilance from all in leadership. These things need to be "nipped in the bud", and our church must not be seen as an easy target. We are grateful that we tackled it as soon as we got wind of it, and so prevented it going any further than it did. I would hate for any church to pass through this kind of trial. I acknowledge that our case did not include actual fornication with a minor. It was however a "shot across the bow", a warning. A hard and protracted battle!

†CHAPTER 16

Lessons from Counselling and CWR

A round the time when we were having the trial with Kim, a member of the King's Church addressed our fraternal. Sarah wanted to set up a Crisis Pregnancy Centre that drew helpers from across the churches in Hailsford. I was so impressed with her presentation that I invited her to address our church during a Sunday morning service. Clare warmed to her immediately, and despite her workload as a teacher, she offered to be trained as a crisis pregnancy counsellor. The centre was set up in the top floor of the new Christian Book Shop which came under the auspices of Hailsford Churches Together. Pastor Alex was a trustee until his retirement and then I accepted the offer to replace him. It was a very professional service that brought glory to God. It also gave Clare and I the privilege and joy of working together with wonderful Christians from other churches.

As the service expanded Clare was asked to help train the new counsellors. Her encounters with women facing an unwanted or unplanned pregnancy are for her to talk about. What I do know is that on our recent sabbatical we returned to our church in Hailsford for a Sunday morning service. After the service Clare was approached by two young ladies who showed her their children whom they did not abort after Clare had counselled them. The icing on the cake was that they were now committed Christians!

The need soon arose for post-abortion trauma counselling and Sarah chose Clare to be the first to go through training. A couple of others followed, including Sarah herself. This was a whole new ball-game and Clare soon realised that a host of other issues were bedfellows of this trauma. She led her first client to a commitment to our Saviour and forgiveness that heals the broken heart. But she wanted further counselling training.

Clare and I were great fans of the Christian writer and counsellor Selwyn Hughes. His book *Marriage as God Intended* has long been my favourite on marriage. We also loved reading the daily devotionals *Every Day With Jesus* together before we prayed at night. In those issues we noticed adverts for CWR Counselling Courses. We were becoming less dependent on Clare's wage, so we took the step of faith and enrolled her on the first course – *Introduction to Biblical Counselling*. She loved every minute of it in the luxurious Waverley Abbey House. So we enrolled her on the Certificate Course.

She brought me back a book that was to change my whole approach to ministry. It was called *Boundaries* by Cloud and Townsend. It taught me what and who I was responsible for, and when to say "yes" and when to say "no". I came to realise that I was responsible *towards* people and not *for* them. I was responsible for myself, as was every other adult person. I saw that when the Lord Jesus raised Lazarus from the dead, He was not responsible for the choices some made to believe on Him, *nor* was He responsible for the choices of others to plot to kill Him. Each person who makes a choice is personally responsible for that choice. When I discharged my responsibility given by God – either to preach, teach or advise, what my listeners did with it was their individual responsibility before God. I cannot tell you just how liberating that truth has been to me. At the *Bema* judgement seat of Christ I will give an account of myself. Clare will not give an account for me and I will not give an account for her. And so on. We were not responsible for Jeff's behaviour, nor for Kim's anorexia.

As a pre-requisite to complete her Certificate of Christian Counselling, Clare had to subject herself to being counselled. How I thank the Lord for His gracious and observable work done in her through those sessions. Having completed her Certificate Course Clare went on to complete the Diploma Course. She had begun counselling during this time. To be accredited she needed to go for supervision once a month. Some of us ministers of the Gospel have had to face harrowing issues and it would be wonderful if it was mandatory for us to go for regular supervision too.

† CHAPTER 17

Divorce in the Church

One day I was walking home from the church when I felt the Lord was telling me to send Clare back to South Africa on a visit to her parents. Clare agreed and we soon booked her flights. I wanted her to be there for a maximum of two weeks but try as we did, we could not find a return flight for a further three weeks. It was to be the longest time we have ever been apart during our marriage, and to make it bearable I would phone her every day.

During the stay with her parents Clare's father asked her all about the Christian message. She was so excited to share the Lord Jesus and the salvation He offers all who come to Him in faith. On her last Sunday there her father wore the suit he had worn to our wedding, and he went to church with her for the first time ever. A few months later he took a massive heart attack, was rushed to hospital but died shortly afterwards. The One who has perfect knowledge of the future had indeed sent Clare for the salvation of her dad.

The bad news came two weeks before Clare's return from her parents. In the early evening I received a phone call from Joy. She was near hysterical as she spat out that Phil had left her for Karen. I felt like I had been hit hard in the stomach. I felt winded.

"Karen who?" I asked in anguish.

"My friend Karen!" Joy replied.

Still in shock I said, "You mean Karen S...?"

"Yes!" she said impatiently.

"Is Phil there?" I asked.

"Yes!"

"I am coming right now to see you both!" I promised as I reached for my car keys. How I wished then that Clare was with me.

As I was finding a parking space outside their home, Phil rushed past me to climb into his car. I wound my window down and asked him where he was going – I wanted to talk to him. He told me that Joy needed me right then and that he would see me the next day. Frustrated I told him to be in my office at 10am the next morning. With that he sped away.

Joy met me at the door and ushered me in. She then sat on her legs in her armchair in a huddle. She was heartbroken, her eyes bloodshot from her weeping. I, too, was heartbroken – and for what seemed a long time, we were both speechless.

It all seemed worse than when I received the news that Clive and Stacy had split up. I guess I felt this way because both Phil and Joy were in leadership, and they had both contributed to the life and outreach of the church perhaps more than any other couple.

"Karen told me that I was the best friend she had ever had!" Joy said as she broke the silence. She was now looking blankly at the door into the hallway. After a few moments she looked forlornly back at me and said, "How could she have done this to me? How could Phil have fallen for her? John, it is just unbelievable." Then the tears flowed freely again. I too began to cry.

I eventually told Joy that I would be seeing Phil in the morning, and that, with God's wisdom and help, I would be doing my best to persuade him to keep his marriage vows to her no matter what the cost to him.

"Thanks John! I know that you will do all you can," she said composing herself. But her composure did not last long. She just could not answer the question "Why?" And neither could I. After some time I asked Joy permission to pray, and both she and I prayed for the miracle needed to save their marriage.

After my visit to Joy I went around to see Karen and her husband Jacob. Karen became very emotional as soon as I was ushered into their lounge by Jacob who had met me at the door. He seemed very accepting of everything which surprised me greatly. "All I want is for Karen to be happy," he told me whilst I waited for her to compose herself.

"Jacob has been a very good husband, and an excellent father," Karen ventured. "I honestly cannot fault him. But I have fallen in love with Phil. I have never felt this way for any other man. I hope you understand Pastor John. I am madly in love with Phil!" Then she looked away and tearfully said, "I don't know what to think concerning Joy. She was my best friend ever. I have betrayed her. I know she loves Phil...in her way. How can I be doing this to her? She has only been good to me...and for me. Here I am...taking Phil from her!" She stopped to blow her nose and wipe her eyes.

"You do not have to go through with this Karen!" I said looking intently at her. "Your promises to Jacob on your wedding day supersede any promises you have made to Phil!"

"There is no point in trying to persuade me, Pastor John. Thanks for trying anyway," she interjected.

"She's right, Pastor John," said Jacob. "Once Karen has made up her mind about something, nothing and no one can change it."

I was beginning to wonder whether Jacob was just resigned to the inevitable, or whether he wished her out of his life for whatever reasons. They both told me of the history of affairs and divorce in their family. I was bewildered. When I could say no more I asked permission to pray for them.

"So long as you do not pray a biased prayer," pleaded Karen to my great surprise.

"My bias is not for any individual involved in these events. My bias is for marriage itself," I replied. I was given permission to pray and I left with Karen sobbing, and Jacob comforting her.

Phil kept his appointment with me the next morning. He was on time despite an obvious reluctance to explain himself to his pastor and friend. I patiently listened as he explained his decision. He no longer had any feelings for Joy. He did not wish her any harm. He no longer wanted to share his life with her. On the other hand, he was deeply in love with Karen. He had never felt this way about a woman before. Their relationship was vibrant and thrilling. Even if he was to take his family to live in Scotland, or even New Zealand, he would never be able to get Karen off his mind or out of his heart. He hardly made eye contact with me throughout his explanation. Meanwhile I was feeling every hope of a reconciliation was evaporating into thin air.

I believe Phil was grateful that I at least listened to him. When he had finished he shook his head as he exclaimed, "I know what you are going to say!" I told him that I would have loved to have had the opportunity to counsel him and Joy had I known that their marriage was in trouble. I said that I felt that if Karen had not shown interest in him he would have made a go of his marriage – like he had made a go of so many other things in his life. I told him that I was heart-broken at the turn of events. I loved him. He had been the best right-hand man I ever had the joy of working with in church life. I loved Joy, Karen and Jacob too.

I told him that his decision to leave Joy for Karen was a very costly decision. Had he counted the cost? He told me that he knew it would be harmful to their two beautiful children but that he would do his best to minimise that harm. He would never belittle their mother to them. He also knew that Karen's child would suffer. Karen's husband was very accepting of her choice and would be allowed full access to their daughter.

He knew that this decision would mean walking away from our church, and he deeply regretted that. He hoped God Himself would understand – after all it did not come as a surprise to Him.

Phil was now keen to leave, but before he rose from his chair I said, "Phil, you have four justifications to make. First you need to justify your decision to Joy. She genuinely loves you and is heart-broken not only at your decision, but also because she keenly feels the betrayal of her friend Karen."

"Joy is a strong person, Pastor John, and she will get over this!"

"Maybe," I replied, "just maybe! Second, you need to justify your decision to family and friends. That is relatively easy as you can say that divorce is all too common in society. Then you will need to justify it to your children. That will be much harder. It will cost you their respect! Finally," I said looking him straight in the eyes, "you will need to justify your actions to the Lord Jesus Christ! He will tell you that He united you with Joy on your wedding day. He will also tell you that He was always there to help you in your marriage."

"As I told you before," Phil interjected, "I believe He will understand. And He is compassionate, isn't He? Anyway...I'll take my chances." By now he was standing and turning to go. We both walked to the door in silence. I opened the door for him, he brushed by me without looking at me, and he walked down the stairs. I said, "Goodbye Phil," as tears rolled down my cheeks. The thought crossed my mind that this was what it could have been like for the father to watch his prodigal son walk away from home.

I walked back to my chair and dropped to my knees. I do not know how long I spent there praying with my understanding and praying in the Spirit. All I know is that I was weak with emotional exhaustion. And so very heartbroken!

A week later Phil phoned to ask in a business tone whether he could begin to build the ramp that would wrap around half the church to enable wheelchair access to our front door. I had given my word to him before and felt I could not spoil my integrity despite the big change in our relationship. Meanwhile I was phoning Joy nearly every day to see how she was coping. She was not coping very well. She was not as strong as he had said she would be. I told her that I had given him the go-ahead for the ramp construction. She felt that he would come to his senses soon, and that I should keep the door open to him. She did question whether she should remain in the worship group, and on the leadership team. I told her that we would really want her to remain in post and that it would be good for her. I lent her Dr James Dodson's wonderful book *Love Must Be Tough* which she found very helpful. Outwardly she maintained her dignity. Inwardly she was falling apart.

I desperately wanted Clare to be by my side. I refrained from telling her the bad news until she safely returned home from South Africa. Then when we were alone I welled up with emotion, struggling to get the words out to tell her. She wrapped her arms around me and asked, "What's making you so upset John?" I told her I did not tell her in my daily phone calls to her because I did not want to spoil her time with her parents. She was very upset with the news and the next day we both met with Joy to console and encourage her. Clare's counselling skills proved invaluable.

I wrote a letter to Phil and Karen. I told them at the beginning of the letter that I valued them and their massive (especially Phil's) contribution to our church family. I assured them that it was not easy for me to write what I was about to write. I knew that it was not my place to judge them, but I knew that one day the Word of God would judge them. Then I wrote that I felt it my duty as their former pastor to share with them a number of Scripture verses relating to adultery and divorce. I wrote that I trusted the Scriptures to speak for themselves.

Phil replied to my letter. He acknowledged that it must have been hard for me to write what I did. He thanked me for being true to God's Word in everything. Then he asked me to please leave them alone to work things out for themselves.

Phil finished the ramp, thus completing the magnificent renovations he had so ably managed. He then sent me the final invoice. It was far more than originally quoted. I reasoned that he had saved us ten times that amount whilst managing the rest of the project, so I did not begrudge him the amount demanded now. However we did not have it all in the bank. So I asked our treasurer for what we could afford, and I sent that to Phil with a promise that the rest would be forthcoming as soon as God provided. Karen replied to that with threats of legal action. So I raided my own savings account and sent them a personal cheque. The church paid me back later.

That was an awful trial! Phil went on to divorce Joy and married Karen. Contrary to predictions, the marriage has worked. I do not know whether I could have handled things differently from the beginning to strengthen and save Phil and Joy's marriage. We had run the "Marriage Course" which they had attended. One summer we had our usual outreach in the Hailsford Park at the Hailsford Festival. Phil had been heavily involved in the preparations. When the weekend arrived he phoned to ask me to relieve him of any duty – he wanted "and needed" to spend time with his family. I had told him that I understood and would cover for him.

The next week I had visited them to see if I could help. I told them then that they could have as much "time off" as they needed to build their family. We went through all their involvements in church and social life, trying to see what was best to cut out. In the end they had convinced me that they did not want to cut back on anything! Perhaps I should have been afraid for their marriage then. Perhaps I should have prayed more specifically and earnestly for their marriage. I do not believe in involvement in church meetings and events during the week that take husbands from their wives, parents from their children, and Christians from their friends and neighbours. Perhaps I should have taught more about balance – the lesson God taught me when I first began in His ministry. I know that no one is indispensable. My grief was exacerbated by my strong feelings at the time that Phil was irreplaceable. His departure left the whole church the poorer, let alone Joy and their two children.

That trial was followed by Dennis' suicide, and a dear member being misinformed about me. He failed to verify the facts with me before passing on that misinformation to another very dear couple.

It all lead to their departure from our lives. That couple had blessed us hugely in their friendship and financial generosity. They say trials come in three's!

†CHAPTER 18

Lessons about
False Teachings

Early on in my ministry I approached a long-serving missionary to ask him what I was to do with teachings I felt were false. Should I tackle them in my sermons, or at my Bible Studies? I will never forget his advice. "We do not have the time to tackle heresy," he said. "We should devote our time to preaching and teaching the truth as we see it in Scripture, and praying that the Holy Spirit will lead our members *'into all truth'*. *If you fill their hearts and minds with truth, there will be no room for error.*"

For most of my ministry I have taken his advice. On the occasions when I have tackled error that is "appealing" or very close to the truth, I have found some of my warnings were counter-productive. The less committed folk have "investigated" themselves, and some have left us for what they have now found to be "more appealing". A positive tone has proven to be much more fruitful than a negative one. That same missionary also told me, "John, I have seen things come, and I have seen them go. Only the truth endures forever!"

Looking back on our decades in His ministry I have also seen things come, and I have seen them go. I have so often backed off when a fellow Christian has differed strongly from me, because I'd rather keep a relationship with them than fall out over something

I judge to be temporary. There has been such a clamour for "things new" that little and not-so-little heresies have "spoiled the vine".

At the first conference that I attended after the start of my ministry I went into the bookshop that had been set up for the conference delegates. On a small TV was an American preacher strutting up and down waving his big leather-bound new looking and open Bible. I did not recognise him nor hear what he was saying. I just winced when I saw him slam his open Bible on his lectern. Then I felt a nausea come over me and I beat a hasty retreat out of the room. I cannot say I heard an audible voice – it was more an inner intuition. I felt the Lord was telling me, "I want you to have nothing to do with that man!" Later I enquired of the convener who "that man" was.

He and his teachings became very popular in Southern Africa. Many Pentecostal and Charismatic ministers left their denominations because of this "new thing God was doing". So I prayed and fasted about how to discern what was truth and what was error. I honestly felt that God gave me a yardstick which I have used ever since with "all things new". *"You will know them by their fruit.* If a teaching *or emphasis* leads to *humility and Christ-centredness* it is *truth.* If a teaching *or emphasis* leads to *arrogance* and *self-centredness* it is *error."*

It has been a big trial to me to have some of my church members leave to experience in another church doctrine or emphasis that has taken them from the humility and Christ-centredness they began with. The Lord Jesus' first teaching was on humility – in fact the Beatitudes are the best description anywhere of a humble person.

I will give you a few examples:

As soon as we arrived in Harare I heard that an old friend of mine, Pastor Simon, preaching in a big church up the road, had berated my church and denomination. I phoned him to say that I felt deeply disappointed and even betrayed by what he allegedly said in his sermon. He arranged to visit me. Within minutes of arriving at our home he launched a full-on verbal assault. He not only attacked my church leaders and denomination, but told me how stupid I was to take on the church for them. He was enthusiastic about the so-called "Prosperity Gospel", and he warned me to "get a life" and go for it too! By the time he was finished with me I felt not only minced into tiny pieces, but also disdainfully swept under the carpet. He then climbed into his shiny new BMW and sped away.

Seven years later Pastor Paul excitedly told me that Pastor Simon had been transformed by a visit to a revival in Mauritius. He was now assisting a Pastor in Bulawayo. The revival had resulted from the preaching of Jesus Christ and Him crucified. Pastor Simon admitted to Pastor Paul that for seven years he had not preached one sermon on the Cross of Christ. Instead he had memorised sermons by American "Word of Faith" or "Prosperity Gospel" preachers, and preached those. He even preached those sermons with an American accent! He was ashamed to recall that he had judged the effectiveness of his sermons not by how many were converted through them, but by the amount of money he squeezed out of the gullible audiences. For some reason Pastor Paul felt that I would be especially pleased to hear of Pastor Simon's repentance and transformation. I was! I met Pastor Simon in our bank when I was organising our finance to move to the UK. We greeted each other like the best of friends. I was thrilled!

Liz asked me to speak to her friend who was so disillusioned with church that she had "given up on God". A meeting in Liz's home was arranged and this is how the conversation went:

"Can you tell me why you are disillusioned with church and God?" I asked.

"I have been through a messy divorce that has left me with very little money," she began. "Well the preacher guaranteed that if I sowed into his ministry all that I had, I would reap a hundredfold. He quoted the Bible that says *'whatever you sow you will reap'*! So I gave him every last cent that I had. That was months ago. I am still waiting to reap. Either he misquoted the Bible or the Bible is *not true*."

"I tell you which verse he quoted," I replied. "Galatians 6:7 says, *'Do not be deceived, God is not mocked; for whatever a man sows, that he will also reap.'*"

"That's the one!" she exclaimed. "It is not *true*, is it." Her tone was now sarcastic.

"I tell you what he has done," I said calmly. "He has taken this verse out of context. Peter says that some of Paul's writings 'are hard to be understood, which untaught and unstable people *twist or wrench out of context, to their own destruction, as they do also the rest of the Scriptures'* (2 Peter 3:16). The context of *'whatever a man sows, that he will also reap'* is in the very next verse which says, *'For he who sows to his flesh will of the flesh reap corruption, but he who sows to the Spirit will of the Spirit reap everlasting life'*. I suggest to you that if you were sowing money in order to get more money, you were *'sowing to the flesh'*."

"That makes perfect sense!" she told me.

"You said that the preacher guaranteed you would reap money in return?" I asked.

"Yes, he guaranteed that!"

"Next time you hear a preacher guarantee anything you must get him to put it in writing," I replied.

She then told me other teachings she had heard in that church that had troubled her. In every case I could point out how the preacher had taken his teaching out of context, or put the emphasis in the wrong place. She became a very faithful member of our fellowship.

I learned that even the wonderful teaching of "who I am in Christ" can lead to arrogance and self-centredness, instead of humility and Christ-centredness, if the *emphasis* is on the "I" and not on "Christ".

———————

Clare had a very good friend called Wendy. Her husband David was a Pentecostal pastor who began in the ministry at the same time as I did. Her children were the same age as ours. When we moved to Harare David and Wendy moved to Mutare. Whilst there Wendy had her third child. This little one was about two years old when Wendy began to experience breathing difficulties. Eventually she had a chest X-ray and the doctors discovered a huge cancerous growth in her chest. They did what they could for her but it was not enough.

So Wendy returned, with David and their three children, to her missionary parents in Harare. Much prayer was offered up for her but to no avail. She kept deteriorating. David would not countenance any talk of her dying, so she loved Clare's frequent visits because she could ask her the tough questions like, "Who will look after my children? No one could love them as much as I do. Why can't I speak to Dave about dying? Why is God not healing me?"

It was a real trial for Clare to watch this special friend in so much physical, emotional and spiritual agony.

A few days before the Lord Jesus stood up from His throne to welcome her home, David took her in a wheelchair to a large church gathering. The two pastors there made a big deal about praying for her. I put praying in italics because it was much more *commanding* and *taking authority over*. They triumphantly "saw" the demons of cancer leave her body. And to the wild excitement of the thousand or so people there, Wendy was declared completely healed.

In honour of Clare's ministry to his wife, a distraught David asked me to be one of the pall-bearers of Wendy's coffin. We brought her coffin to the front of her father's church, and as I helped position it in front of the pulpit I looked up at the balcony to see those two pastors there. I wondered what must have been going through their minds.

After Brian came to Christ in a private hospital ward, the Lord graciously partially healed him from his spinal injuries (someone had whacked him across the back with a metal pole). He was healed enough to enable him to come hobbling to church each Sunday. A well-meaning Christian friend began to give him books on healing. All sorts of formulae were offered to him to secure his healing. He was to quote healing Scriptures over himself, such as *"by His stripes I was healed"*. Whenever I asked him how he was he would say "I am healed!", and he would continue to lean on his special stick as he dragged himself to his chair. It reminded me of a story that a university friend of mine told me. He was sitting in the Pietermaritzburg Town Hall waiting to hear a Christian Science speaker when a person using walking sticks plumped herself down in the vacant seat next to him. Pointing to her sticks she said, "Those are not real. They are imaginary!"

So I looked to the Lord for a sermon on Divine Healing. It is my conviction that Divine healing is a Sovereign act of God. There are no formulas. We are not in the position to judge why He chooses to heal some and not to heal others. It is His prerogative. And He tells us to call for the elders to pray for us when we are sick (James 5:14,15). We must say we are sick when we are! I spoke of my concern for people who go for prayer for a condition, to be told, if they are not instantly healed, that either they have sin or they have a lack of faith. They then leave the altar with two problems instead of the one they went for prayer for. Some have given up on God because of this insensitive approach. At the end of that sermon Brian responded to the appeal. When Pastor Daniel and I approached him he was weeping. I asked him the matter.

"I want to repent," he sobbed.

"Repent of what?" we asked.

"Repent of trying to heal myself, instead of trusting the Lord to do it for me!"

I had not put it that way in my sermon, so I knew God was speaking to him. We had the whole church join hands as Pastor Daniel and

I laid ours on Brian's head. He still needed his walking stick to leave the church, but that night he was back without it! The next day he returned to his physiotherapist who had given him his final assessment the Friday before. Brian insisted on another assessment, and he was declared healed. His physiotherapist began coming to our church as a result of a Sovereign act of an Almighty God.

We had the privilege of hearing Anne Graham Lotz, daughter of Billy Graham, preach at one of our Bible Weeks. During her sermon she said, "When you see what so-called Pentecostals get up to on some of our Christian TV channels you can understand why mainstream Christianity wants none of it!" I sadly agree! I am a passionate believer in the Baptism with the Holy Spirit. My infilling on the 13th June, 1971, both humbled and Christ centred me. I wanted the experience they had at the beginning (Acts 11:15), I still want what happened in the New Testament. I revere and I am in awe of the precious Holy Spirit. Only by His gracious working in our lives can the life of Jesus Christ shine forth. Only by His fruit and gifts can we adequately represent Jesus Christ to a lost and hell-bound world. He is never a plaything or a slave, nor will He be ordered about by any of us.

The lessons I have learned are to stand foursquare on God's infallible and ever-relevant Word; to *"Test all things;"* and *"hold fast what is good"* (1 Thessalonians 5:21); and to be like Paul who told the Ephesian Church elders *"I have not shunned to declare to you the whole counsel of God"* (Acts 20:27).

†CHAPTER 19

Financial Battles

I have written a whole chapter in *Privileged Witness* about the wonderful ways God has provided for us throughout our ministry. However, I believe He wanted all along to have provided more. Let me explain through an amazing story told us by Linda, wife of Pastor Alan, my best friend in Harare. When they were at *Christ for all Nations* Bible Institute in Dallas, Texas, Linda wanted to buy a good birthday present for Alan. She saw a camera in a shop window costing $99.99 and felt that it would be a perfect present for him. He could capture memories of friends and places there in Dallas before their return to Zimbabwe. Their budget was very tight and so she asked God to provide the $99.99 needed. That was a week before Alan's birthday. No money came from anywhere. Linda was very disappointed as she was sure God had heard her prayer, and that He wanted Alan to have the camera.

A week after Alan's birthday Linda received a letter from a Christian friend in Canada. In it was a cheque for $100. What was so remarkable about this gift was that it was accompanied by an apology. He wrote that he had felt God prompt him two weeks before to send Linda the $100 enclosed. He was asking her to forgive him if the delay in his obedience had caused her any distress! She went out immediately to purchase the camera.

In all of my Christian walk I have never known financial assistance to fall from heaven. It has always come through people on earth! That is obvious. However, I do not believe that it is obvious to all our church members. I believe God's plans to provide for us were often thwarted by other's lack of sensitivity to His prompting, just plain disobedience, or lack of integrity to keep promises. Here are some examples from this battlefield:

We discovered that the Harare church was $3000 in debt and could not afford a salary for us, let alone pay our relocation costs from Redcliff. I asked Pastor Charles, and he told me to look to the Lord, and not to him. It seemed that he was frustrated that I still had not "got the message" to look to God for the meeting of all my needs. So I resorted to earnest prayer and I booked the furniture removals in faith. Just before the removals date I received a phone call from Pastor Jonathan in Bulawayo. He was the Zimbabwe Church Treasurer. He asked me how much I needed to relocate to Harare and promised the full amount. The Lord had come through for us. We were very grateful indeed.

We arrived in Harare and settled into the manse. That Sunday Pastor Bob was back to induct us into the ministry there. To our surprise fifty people came to our first service. That was more than twice as many as we were leaving in Redcliff and Kwe Kwe. My mother, my two brothers and their wives were there, plus some friends of Pastor Bob. He preached another wonderful sermon, and at the end called on all those who would support Clare and I to stand to their feet. All stood. He commended them all to God's grace in prayer and closed the service. Before he left us to it the next day, he warned me to not take on a treasurer until the financial situation had improved substantially and consistently. "Treasurers can buckle under the pressure of 'cash-flow issues'," he concluded.

The following Sunday we were down to about twenty. My heart sank. This was the second church we were to rescue from the brink. It was going to be hard. It would keep us on our knees. Pastor Sidney phoned to tell me that he would return the church car as soon as he found a replacement for himself and two weeks later he returned it – with an empty tank of fuel! Whilst visiting my brother in a nearby village I mentioned selling the church car to help clear our church debt. He knew someone there needing a car and shortly afterwards Fred bought it for $3000. I banked it and cleared our debt. However, within a week of buying the car I received a phone-call complaining that the hydraulic suspension had collapsed, and that Fred wanted his money back. I was plunged into a crisis because the bank had withdrawn their overdraft facility for the church. In answer to prayer a friend of Fred offered to fix his car for nothing, and it turned out to be a reliable car for many more years. We managed (just) on donations from the few left in the church.

I did not enjoy filling in as treasurer, and as soon as the finance became steady, I appointed a treasurer. The salary policy was for the pastor to receive the average of the working men in the congregation. We never achieved this noble aim, but we did get by. I remember our first holiday from Harare. I had a budget and asked God to make up $150 to meet it. Just before our departure date I was speaking at a meeting at Norton village. After the meeting I was handed an envelope containing cash. As I received it I commented "$150?" Tears appeared in the donor's eyes as he nodded. When I told him of my request to God for that amount, he was quite overwhelmed that he had been so sensitive to God's prompting. I was so grateful for another answer to prayer.

Our treasurer, Susan, was only in post for three months before we suffered a setback. It was December and our congregation were slow in placing their tithes and gifts into the tithe box. This meant that there was no money to pay me a wage. Susan freaked. She told me that she felt guilty enough that my wage was so low, but to give me no wage before Christmas was just too much for her. She resigned, and I took back her job. Pastor Bob's warning came true and I regretted having been too hasty in appointing a treasurer – and especially one so sensitive as Susan. I learned a big lesson then. I was grateful when the money did come in after Christmas, and I was also grateful that Susan did not leave the church. When our eldest son was in primary school and our middle son in pre-school Clare went back to teaching. Her wage greatly relieved the financial pressure we had been under for so many years. I loved looking after our youngest son until he too was going to pre-school.

I still clearly remember a very vivid dream I had early on in Harare. I dreamed that as I was greeting people in the car park before a Sunday morning service a big new Mercedes Benz pulled up, and a very well dressed gentleman emerged. I greeted him and he took a seat in the middle of the church. Whilst I was preaching I noticed that he was taking notes, and looking up each passage of the Bible that I quoted. After the service he asked to have a word with me. "I believe that the Lord wants me to attend this church from now on. I also believe that He wants me to pay you *up to* $1000 a sermon depending how good it is. I will begin that next week."

I protested, saying that we do not do things like that in our church. He was not prepared to debate, and I could easily tell that he would be true to his promise. "Up to $1000 a sermon!" I was not even earning that per month. Soon enough it became more a desire to score ten out of ten for my sermon. All night I thought about his promise, and early Monday morning I began searching for a good theme for my next Sunday sermon. I knew that it would need to be well prepared ... and well practiced. Then I realised that it would need to carry God's blessing. If it was to be a sermon from God's heart through my heart to this man's heart, I would need the anointing of the Holy Spirit Himself! That meant prayer and even fasting. That is when I awoke from my sleep. It was then that God challenged me on motive! That dream, whenever I am reminded of it, has continued to challenge me on motive for preaching, and everything to do with the ministry!

Nevertheless one of the biggest pressures on me was the pressure to hold on to church members. We were blessed in Redcliff/Kwe Kwe,

Harare, and Hailsford with fabulous churches with very good ministry. If a member felt he could be better fed elsewhere he too often would move on. If I offended him in my preaching or pastoring, he could possibly move on. Even if there were problems in the church family, he could move on. If he failed to find good friends we could also lose him. On top of all that there was the awful problem of emigration from Zimbabwe. When a member left for whatever reason, we would lose his financial contributions. One of our members was a doctor. His tithe paid my whole wage. I was delighted as we were building a church in Chitungwisa and needed money from our church for that. One day he phoned me, complaining about a few things. When he rang off I fell to my knees by our bed.

"What's going on?" Clare asked.

"I fear Dr Robin is about to announce his departure from our church," I replied. Within minutes he phoned back to tell me that he was leaving the church, and that his tithe would come to an end at the end of the month. He told me that the reason was I had been to visit him and not noticed that his marriage was falling apart. I remember the last visit to his home. There was tension in their marriage and I did try to lead them into a discussion about it but they resisted. They did not ask for help. I closed the visit in prayer for them both, and had prayed since for God's blessing on their marriage. Their departure left a big hole in our finances. God saw the need and within the month a farmer began to tithe the same amount as Dr Robin. That was a wonderful answer to prayer, even if it was a very sad blow to lose them.

Towards the end of our time in Hailsford we were blessed to have Calum and Sue in our church. Theirs was a "rags to riches" story. We had stuck with them through very hard times, so when they got on their feet and began to really prosper, they took special care to bless us financially. They sold us their family car for £1 when they bought their first Mercedes Benz. They sponsored us to visit my brother in New Zealand. They gave us thousands of pounds during our first sabbatical. He was doing so well that he promised us that when he sold his shares in his company he would give us one million US dollars. When he was buying a new much bigger home he dropped big hints that he would sell us his present home "for what we could afford". Wonderful promises which, based on past record, we really believed. Then came a fateful night when a friend of his passed on information to him which made him doubt my integrity. Despite explaining carefully that the information was taken completely out of context or chronology, Calum and Sue left the church and rescinded their promises. Once again God needed to teach me not to look to any man – my eyes were to be always fixed on the Author and Finisher of my faith, who had endured the cross, and such hostility of sinners against Himself (Hebrews 12:2,3). The greatest loss was our close friendship with them. We really loved and appreciated them, and had been through so many trials together which had added to that bond.

Others have also made wonderful promises to Clare and I which they did not fulfil. I wished for their sakes that they had never made them. I pray I'll have learned a great lesson to never make promises unless I am absolutely sure I can fulfil them to the letter. I pray God will always enable me to hold on to my integrity. I admit that I am not blameless in regard to keeping promises. However I have discovered the wonderful power of confession, sincere apology and explanation (not excuse).

I have also learned that when a person needs legitimate financial help I must give it to them without any expectation that they will pay me or the church back (Luke 6:35). This is because someone who has promised to pay back may begin to avoid you, and even break off their relationship with you, if they cannot afford to pay it all back. So I tell them that if they want to, and can afford to pay it back in the future, they must please put it secretly into the Tithes Box. I believe that I have saved many a relationship by making those "terms and conditions" clear.

Before we went to Hailsford from Harare we were asked by the UK church executive to raise the money for our airfare and they would reimburse us when we landed at Heathrow. They never kept that promise, even though they could easily afford to. Instead they gave us £500 settling-in allowance. The salary policy of the UK denomination was to pay a wage below the threshold for paying income tax, and to provide a home rent-free. Our new church had money in the bank and could have afforded twice what we were paid, but the church in Leeds had no such surplus and it was considered unfair that I received more than the pastor there could. My budget for my family of five, after paying my tithe and utilities, was a meagre £15 a day – or £3 each. You can imagine how buying a pair of trainers for one of our sons could blow our budget. On top of that Britain was in a recession, and Clare could not find work to subsidise the church. Her Southern African qualifications were not recognised by the Local Education Authority so the most she could get was a little supply teaching, which she hated.

I bought our groceries from the cheapest shop, going for all the special offers. Clare and I fasted often in those days and not always for spiritual reasons. We were trapped with no money to return to Zimbabwe. What a horrible and protracted battle. To add insult to injury, the hierarchy accused me of being "greedy" when I asked for an increase. I told them the policy in Zimbabwe (of an average wage of the working men in the congregation) to be told, "Well we do not have that policy in Britain."

After three years of severe financial trial I listened to tape recordings of the General Superintendent of a denomination in Australia. He believed that the drop-out of the ministry in Australia was primarily because of the low value attached to pastors as reflected in their appallingly low wages. The philosophy of the churches seemed to be "Lord, You keep him humble and we'll keep him poor!" He had introduced an Australian teacher's wage structure, believing that no Australian believed a teacher was overpaid! Since then the denomination experienced unprecedented growth.

I also asked the National Treasurer of a large UK denomination about the wage structure in his denomination. He told me that they once had a ridiculous situation where they had a very low wage for every Pastor, no matter that their congregation could pay them considerably more. He then said that there was a prophecy warning them that if they did not repent of this, and look after their pastors in their wages, God would close the denomination down. God blessed them when they not only left it up to the local church session to determine the wage of their pastor, but they also gave a very fair set of salary recommendations every year for those sessions to aim for or exceed. For those churches that struggled to pay their pastor a decent living wage, this denomination had a Pastoral Care Fund to call upon. That produced growth here in the UK and in their missions department.

I was all for our small denomination being absorbed into that one. Years later I joined it myself and am delighted. I deeply regret not joining when we first arrived in the UK.

As soon as I could I abolished the practice of passing an offering basket around the congregation at every service. I wanted to see not-yet-Christians coming to hear the Gospel of Jesus Christ without being asked to pay for it before hearing the message. The Lord Jesus watched over a box at the entrance to the Temple. I was confident He would do the same in our church. I also wanted the giving to be as much "in secret" as possible. I have always been a strong believer in tithing, and giving as He leads. Giving to Him is an act of worship which is best done without coercion and in secret. Since reading about George Muller and the orphanages he acquired by faith alone, I have aspired to trust God in prayer for my needs, rather than ask others.

In Hailsford I inherited a treasurer. He was a very amicable person and I had no problem trusting him with the finances. It must have been two whole years before I noticed, to my horror, that as he walked out of the church he would unlock the Tithe Box, grab the contents in his hand, and stuff them into his pocket. Not wanting to make a scene, I confronted him on a "pastoral visit". I told him that the money needed to be counted by two trusted members and recorded with their signatures, before he took it off to be banked.

"This is how it is done in the UK, Pastor John. What is it with you? Do you not trust me?"

"Of course I trust you!" I replied as I began to doubt the sincerity of my words. "I want the system we employed in Zimbabwe for *your* protection, and *not* the protection of the money."

He remained unconvinced and refused to comply. He was usually in a hurry to return home to his "not-yet-Christian" wife, and he would not wait around for others to do what he was fully capable and trustworthy to do himself. So I took the matter to our new General Overseer. He wholeheartedly endorsed my procedure, saying it was correct and common practice throughout the churches in the UK for two people to record the offerings. I then looked more carefully at the monthly bank statements. Our treasurer was a great advocate of congregation members paying by standing order – it helped him budget. Yet there was no record of a standing order in his name. I asked him about this anomaly. That infuriated him and he resigned as treasurer on the spot. He also left the church. That really upset me.

I appointed a new treasurer who followed the right procedures and God blessed us, so much so that our income more than doubled each year for the next three years. Our new General Superintendent also did away with the low wage structure in the denomination, allowing the local leadership to determine how much they could afford to pay their pastor. So my wage also increased substantially. With that I could at least pay income tax! I was grateful for dignity restored, I always want to pay towards services like education, law and order and health! The local leadership also paid me the acceptable mileage allowance instead of a flat (inadequate) monthly car allowance as before. I kept a careful record of "business" mileage. If I was given cash for conducting a funeral, wedding or if I was given a gratuity for preaching in another church, I would always add that to my wage for income tax purposes. I also availed myself of the services of a godly accountant to do my tax returns. I, too, wanted to be blameless and above reproach so as to have God's good pleasure and blessing.

We have been so blessed! We are buying our own home now that will be completely ours by the time we retire. We have two reliable cars and our home is well kitted out. We have afforded holidays, visits to our family, and a life-changing tour of the Holy Land which was a dream for decades. We have three godly sons, three godly daughters-in-law, and six wonderful grandchildren. We are blessed by God's amazing grace – His unmerited favour. We worship and adore Him!

I look back now at Pastor Charles' insistence that I trust God for everything and not look to any man. I now thank him for that stand, although at the time I thought he was uncaring. At least this way we have so many testimonies in the midst of our many trials. The middle verse in the Bible says, 'It is better to trust in the Lord, than to put confidence in man,' (Psalm 118:8).

I spoke recently to a church member who was going through a terrible trial. I told her that Clare and I have been through trials that were so difficult that we thought they were the end of the world for us. We could not see ourselves ever getting through them. Yet by God's faithfulness and amazing grace we did. His same faithfulness and amazing grace will see her through too. Within months she shared in church a truly wonderful testimony about getting through an even greater trial.

The Lord Jesus said that He was humble enough and gentle enough to yoke Himself alongside us to pull whatever heavy load is our lot to pull. It is an unequal yoke because we are weak and sometimes foolish. He is all-powerful and all-wise. Oh to have *Him* at our side always! What enduringly blessed fellowship. What sweet and glorious victories along the way. We will have trials, He promised that, *"These things I have spoken to you, that in Me you may have peace. In the world you will have tribulation; but be of good cheer, I have overcome the world,"* (John 16:33). He has also promised triumphs!

> *Now thanks be to God who always leads us in triumph in Christ, and through us diffuses the fragrance of His knowledge in every place. For we are to God the fragrance of Christ among those who are being saved and among those who are perishing. To the one we are the aroma of death leading to death, and to the other the aroma of life leading to life. And who is sufficient for these things? For we are not, as so many, peddling the word of God; but as of sincerity, but as from God, we speak in the sight of God in Christ*
> (2 Corinthians 2:14–17)

†CHAPTER 20

Triumphs in the Midst of the Battlefield

Our greatest joy has always been the salvation of souls. I could tell of many in our time in Redcliff, Harare and Hailsford. How we prayed for more, much more. I have written about several in my book *Privileged Witness*. Here are a few short stories to add to those longer, more detailed ones:

Sylvia was from Slovakia, and was working as an au-pair not far from the church. One Sunday morning she happened to be passing our church as people were entering for the morning service. She felt an urge to join them. As she reached me I stretched out my hand to greet her. With a very timid voice she asked me in her strong Slovak accent whether she was permitted to attend our church. I said, "You are most welcome any time!" She was promptly greeted by a young lady entering at the same time who offered to sit with her during the service.

In her testimony afterwards she told Clare and I that the moment she entered the building she felt God's welcome. She just knew that He had led her there. She had never been in a church service like that before. All the songs were new to her.

After my sermon I gave an "altar call" and to my delight she raised her hand immediately. Within three weeks I had the great joy of baptising her in water and praying for her to be filled with the Holy Spirit. She never missed a service, and she joined our youth group and loved it. When she was about to return to Slovakia after her two years were up, she told her friend Joan that she was welcome to come to the UK, and take her place as au pair, on condition that she came along to our church. Joan did just that and we had the joy of leading her to Christ. She went for evening classes to improve her English, and there she witnessed to fellow Slovakians, three of whom came to our church and gave their lives to Christ! And they were all called Joan! Sylvia joined a Christian Radio Station back in Slovakia. There she met and married a fine Christian man, and the last time I heard about them they were serving the Lord Jesus in Israel.

Colin was a young man who returned to us after Robert's group had left. His identical twin Peter did not, although I had many dealings with him over the years. Colin had a grandmother called Janet who lived with her partner William. Colin witnessed Jesus to them often but they did not respond. He invited them to his church, saying that it had a new minister from Zimbabwe and that he was sure they would like him. However, when William and Janet were on holiday in Malta one year, William damaged his back and was in very serious difficulty. Before going to bed that night he made a pact with God that if He healed his back he would attend Colin's church on his return to Hailsford. Overnight God healed him! So as soon as he returned home he and Janet came to our church with their delighted grandson. Despite my appeals at the end of my sermons neither William nor Janet responded to give their lives to Christ. So I visited them in their flat. My appointment was for 10am and I knocked on their door exactly on time. This small deed greatly impressed William. He told me so! He had been a Sergeant-Major in the British Army and had been used to punctuality and precision! (From that visit onwards

I would ring his bell at precisely the appointed time to find him right there to open the door).

He told me about his pledge to God in Malta and then asked me to explain to him and Janet exactly how to become a "born-again" Christian. I had the great joy of leading them both, that morning, into a relationship with Jesus Christ. Oh joy! About six weeks later, when I was visiting them again, I noticed a fresh photograph of them outside what I recognised to be the Registry Office. I asked them about it. Sheepishly they informed me that they had been living together for thirty years. Immediately after their "born-again" experience they had been convicted that they should get married.

After a couple of years Janet's health began to fail. She had a valve replacement in her heart but still grew weaker. William could not face coming to church without her so my bi-weekly visits became more and more important. I had the privilege of conducting her funeral not long afterwards. We sponsored their grandson Colin through Regent's Theological College, I preached at his wedding to Shu (a South Korean girl), at the Regent's Chapel, and he later acquired an English speaking church in Seoul, the capital of South Korea.

Another couple decided to try our church when they heard our *Church Without Walls* outreach at the Bandstand. They were new to Hailsford and were looking for a church to call their spiritual home. She invited her newly married sister Trish. Trish and Mike both gave their lives to Christ in our church and I had the privilege of baptising them shortly afterwards. All four of them were a wonderful blessing to us all.

I would write in my prayer diary the names of everyone who visited the church. So after Brian and Sarah attended for their first time their names went in my little book. They only came once, yet every week afterwards I prayed for them. About a year later they arrived at the church again. God must have helped me remember their faces. "Brian and Sarah!" I joyfully said as I shook their hands. They told me later that the reason why they were convinced to make our church their spiritual home was me remembering their names! They were even more delighted to hear that in every week in that year I had been praying for them. They had been working for Overseas Missions in Morocco in that year.

Their new job in Hailsford was to manage a fish and chip shop just minutes away from our church. They lived in the flat above the shop. When volunteers from the church worked on the massive renovations of the church on Saturdays, Brian would insist on supplying free fish and chips to every worker! When they sensed our financial hardships they offered to employ Clare to do their ironing and cleaning. Although this was a far cry from teaching, Clare was grateful for the £5 an hour they paid her and we were grateful for the many fish suppers they sent to us as a family! A few years later Brian and Sarah went to Bible College to train for the ministry.

Then there was young Angie, a very spiritual young teenager who told her mother Cathy one day that she needed to go to church to find God. As our church was on their way into town, Angie determined to come, and Cathy came along with her. Angie very quickly grasped the Gospel message and gave her life to Christ. Her enthusiasm for her Saviour made a great impact upon her mother, so soon after Angie's conversion Cathy yielded to Christ's claim to her whole life. They were both baptised together, and I asked Cathy's unbelieving husband to assist me in lowering and raising them up from the water. My efforts to win him to Christ over the following years proved fruitless, yet he fully supported Cathy and Angie in their growing relationship with Christ.

———

Then there was Harry and Felicity. They were South Africans that had recently moved to a small village very near Hailsford. Their one son chose our church as the first church to try out. They came through the doors on the Sunday before we tore out the wooden floors of our main hall to begin our major renovations. It was also the Sunday when Cathy and Angie were baptised. God thoroughly blessed the service that day and it was enough to convince Harry and his family that God had led them to the church that He wanted them in. They became our firm friends and we began a house-group in their home which Clare and I attended. Felicity had a very real gift from God for hospitality and the family proved to be a wonderful blessing to our church.

———

I met Ivan at an outreach our worship band held in a neighbouring town. In talking to him he disclosed that he had been a committed churchman but that his church had folded and he was not attending any church anymore. I told him that he was most welcome to try our church in Hailsford. He brought his lovely wife Alice to our next Sunday service, they both felt at home and they soon committed themselves to being a part of us. When he finally disclosed that he had been first a YWAMer and then the minister of the church that folded, I asked him back into the pulpit. That is when real breakthrough came to his wounded heart. God blessed his preaching, we all loved it, and he became a regular preacher for us. I was later delighted that he accepted the role of elder in our church. Alice, being a primary school teacher, became a terrific asset to our children's work.

I conducted the weddings of three of his beautiful daughters and later had the unspeakable privilege of leading two of them, with their husbands, to Christ. I tell the story in *Privileged Witness* of their eldest daughter's baptism which led to Melvin and Pat's sound conversion.

They brought their plumber Paul to the church, and I had the privilege of leading him and his partner Susanne to Christ, conducting their subsequent wedding, and a couple of years later sadly conducting Susanne's funeral after she lost her battle against lung cancer.

Ivan had a friend John who had been in his church before it folded. He was now separating from his wife and in deep depression. I spent many hours encouraging John and finally he came back to Christ and began attending the King's Church where he had friends. His son Mark, however, warmed to us and began to attend our church. There I had the privilege of leading him to Christ. He wavered in his faith for a while until we baptised him at our annual church Away Weekend. God wonderfully baptised him with the Holy Spirit and his subsequent spiritual growth was exponential. He was taken under Calum and Sue's wing and when he decided to go to Bible College to train for the ministry, Calum and the church jointly paid all his expenses.

I was asked by a member to visit a client of hers who was dying of cancer. I visited Grace in her home. Her husband James was there too. We talked about her illness and then I asked her whether she was ready to die. She said that she was. Then I asked her whether she was sure that when she died she would be received by the Lord Jesus in heaven. She certainly hoped so. She told me that she had been a good wife, mother and neighbour. If God had a set of scales to judge an individual on merit, the scales would tip in her favour. I offered to share from the Bible how she could be sure. That was when James stepped in to tell me that she was sure. End of discussion! He then began to speak of other things.

I visited Grace and James again, only to have him digress the conversation away from what to me really mattered. Coming away frustrated that evening I called on the Lord to please arrange for me to see Grace on my own. A few days later I met James in the High Street. I asked how Grace was. He told me that she had been admitted to St Luke's Hospital in a nearby town, and that he had been told it would be a matter of days now. Although I expressed my sadness at hearing the news of her prognosis, inwardly I rejoiced that God had answered my prayer. I told him that as a minister I could visit her out of visiting hours, leaving the visiting hours to him and their son to spend time alone with her.

The next morning I made the journey through to St Luke's. Grace was delighted to see me, and soon we were speaking about her dying. Once again she assured me that she had been a good wife, mother and neighbour. She had long given up attending church because of the hypocrisy she found there. I knew that she was telling the truth, yet I also knew that it is *"by grace you have been saved through faith, and that not of yourselves; it is the gift of God, not of works, lest anyone should boast,"* Ephesians 2:8,9. I was determined that this wonderful lady had assurance of her salvation through faith in Christ's merits, and not her own. I was not going to leave her that morning until I had witnessed the great transaction between Saviour and sinner.

I quoted the first and great commandment, *"You shall love the Lord your God with all your heart, with all your soul, with all your mind, and with all your strength,."* Mark 12:30. When I asked her whether she had managed to keep that first commandment she looked away, then bowed her head, then looked back at me, confessing that she had not. As she was reacting to my question, I was in my heart pleading the Blood of Jesus. I know that to plead the Blood of Jesus is to change the plea of guilty to a plea of innocence. It was a spiritual battle that I was determined to win. The Lord Jesus had a claim to Grace by right of purchase. The devil had to let go! When I told her that the Lord Jesus offered her His pardon, she burst into tears. "Please pray for me," she pleaded, "I am a sinner and I need Jesus to pardon me!" The battle was won, Grace prayed the sinner's prayer with me, and her eternity was sealed!

The next morning I met with James. He told me that Grace was transformed by my visit. She knew that when she died she would be welcomed by the Lord Jesus into heaven. She had pleaded with him and their son to ask Jesus to pardon them too. He told me that he was certainly thinking seriously about it now. That afternoon Grace was received by Her Saviour. I had the privilege of conducting her funeral at their local parish church. Forever we will be grateful for the battle won that morning at St Luke's. Sadly I did not win the battle for James or their son, even though they appreciated my ministry to Grace. The great lesson here is that there is a spiritual battle for every soul on earth. It is the Lord's battle and we share in it. The victory is always worth the battle. I feel this battle every time I give an altar call after a Gospel message. It highlights the need for persistent, intentional, corporate and determined prayer.

Every Tuesday for almost ten years I had the enormous privilege of preaching a Gospel Message to inmates at the Gatwick Immigration Detention Centre. When it became a short-term detention centre, with inmates destined to be sent back to their respective countries, my ministry became quite fruitful in terms of new converts and restored backsliders. The average responding to the altar call was two, with the best service yielding ten respondents. Obviously the real test of their meeting with their Saviour there would be their walk with Him afterwards. Heaven alone will tell!

Epilogue

Have the battles been worth it? Most definitely! Romans 8:18 says, *"For I consider that the sufferings of this present time are not worthy to be compared with the **glory** which shall be revealed in us."*

As I have said before, I have learned that the only thing we can take to heaven is people – the rest we will leave behind. As Paul says in 1 Thessalonians 2:19,20, *"For what is our hope, or joy, or crown of rejoicing? Is it not even you in the presence of our Lord Jesus Christ at His coming? For you are our **glory** and joy."*

I could have chosen an easier path by choosing another career. However Christ chose me for His ministry as pastor. 1 Corinthians 1:26–31 says, *"For you see your calling, brethren, that not many wise according to the flesh, not many mighty, not many noble, are called. But God has chosen the foolish things of the world to put to shame the wise, and God has chosen the weak things of the world to put to shame the things which are mighty; and the base things of the world and the things which are despised God has chosen, and the things which are not, to bring to nothing the things that are, that no flesh should glory in His presence. But of Him you are in Christ Jesus, who became for us wisdom from God—and righteousness and sanctification and redemption— that, as it is written, ,He who glories, let him glory in the Lord.'"*

The Lord Jesus warned me through Scripture that it is a hard road. Matthew 5:11,12, *"Blessed are you when they revile and persecute you, and say all kinds of evil against you falsely for My sake. Rejoice and be exceedingly glad, for great is your reward in heaven, for so they persecuted the prophets who were before you."* 2 Timothy 3:12, *"Yes, and all who desire to live godly in Christ Jesus will suffer persecution."* John 16:33, *"These things I have spoken to you, that in Me you may have peace. In the world you will have tribulation; but be of good cheer, I have overcome the world."*

I could have chosen an easier message to preach. Galatians 6:12,14, *"As many as desire to make a good showing in the flesh, these would compel you to be circumcised, only that they may not suffer persecution for the cross of Christ...But God forbid that I should boast except in the cross of our Lord Jesus Christ, by whom the world has been crucified to me, and I to the world."*

I have learned that many of the tribulations have served to make me a better minister of the Gospel. 2 Corinthians 1:3–7, *"Blessed be the God and Father of our Lord Jesus Christ, the Father of mercies and God of all comfort, who comforts us in all our tribulation, that we may be able to comfort those who are in any trouble, with the comfort with which we ourselves are comforted by God. For as the sufferings of Christ abound in us, so our consolation also abounds through Christ. Now if we are afflicted, it is for your consolation and salvation, which is effective for enduring the same sufferings which we also suffer. Or if we are comforted, it is for your consolation and salvation. And our hope for you is steadfast, because we know that as you are partakers of the sufferings, so also you will partake of the consolation."*

I have also learned that trials have served to mature me. James 1:2–4, *"My brethren, count it all joy when you fall into various trials, knowing that the testing of your faith produces patience. But let patience have its perfect work, that you may be perfect and complete, lacking nothing."*

I can honestly and gratefully testify with Paul, *"that all things work together for good to those who love God, to those who are the called according to His purpose. For whom He foreknew, He also predestined to be conformed to the image of His Son, that He might be the firstborn among many brethren,"* (Romans 8:28).

As in the story of Job, God always has the devil on a leash. He can pull him back whenever He chooses. As with the story of Elijah, God knows when *"the journey is too great for you,"* (1 Kings 19:7b). David reminds us that ultimately *"the battle is the Lord's"* (1 Samuel 17:47b); Zechariah 4:6 reminds us *"Not by might nor by power, but by My Spirit, says the Lord of hosts"* and Jesus reminds us in

Matthew 28:18–20, *"All authority has been given to Me in heaven and on earth. Go therefore and make disciples of all the nations, baptising them in the name of the Father and of the Son and of the Holy Spirit, teaching them to observe all things that I have commanded you; and* **lo, I am with you always, even to the end of the age. Amen.***"* He may deliver us from tribulation, or in tribulation, or through tribulation. Throughout He will enable and empower us by the precious Holy Spirit. His grace will prove, time and again, to be sufficient. When we are weak He remains strong – for us! Praise Him! Hallelujah!

We just so want to be able to say with Paul, *"I have fought the good fight, I have finished the race, I have kept the faith. Finally, there is laid up for me the crown of righteousness, which the Lord, the righteous Judge, will give to me on that Day, and not to me only but also to all who have loved His appearing,"* 2 Timothy 4:7,8. There is also a *crown of life* for those who *endure temptation* (James 1:12) and a *crown of glory* for those who faithfully shepherd God's flock through example and service (1 Peter 5:1–4).

Many would not give up what pastors have given up to put up with what they have to put up with so that they can save up what they save up for. Our eyes are on the eternal, and not the temporal.

Other books by John Henson

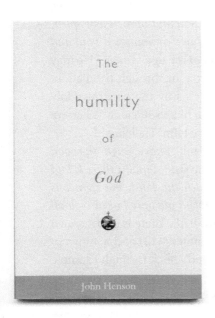

The Humility of God

"A powerful, challenging and moving pen-portrait of the character of Christ that mixes sound theological exegesis with practical pastoral illustration."

John Glass, author of *Building Bigger People*

Privileged Witness

"You will love reading these real life stories which are skillfully and sensitively told throughout this book. John's passion for evangelism is a thread running through every page from start to finish. It will not fail to inspire you, motivate you and warm your heart."

Margaret Peat, author of *The White Elephant* and *The Seagull*

An environmentally friendly book printed and bound in England by www.printondemand-worldwide.com

PEFC Certified

This product is
from sustainably
managed forests
and controlled
sources

www.pefc.org

This book is made of chain-of-custody materials; FSC materials for the cover and PEFC materials for the text pages.